Anonymous

A trip to the English lakes in May 1864

Anonymous

A trip to the English lakes in May 1864

ISBN/EAN: 9783337147068

Printed in Europe, USA, Canada, Australia, Japan

Cover: Foto ©Andreas Hilbeck / pixelio.de

More available books at **www.hansebooks.com**

A TRIP

TO

THE ENGLISH LAKES

IN

MAY, 1864.

BY

A GOURMET.

A TRIP

TO

THE ENGLISH LAKES

IN MAY, 1864.

———◆———

A little' moment, Gourmet, if you please! Banting has rooms in Keswick just now, and I must be there soon; we wish you to join us for a few days, and enjoy the fresh tints of spring in that lovely country. Eh?

Spring, indeed! it's nothing but "blow, blow thou wintry wind,"—ugh! there'll be many a bleak house in Cumberland, I warrant.

Now listen to the plan.

Nonsense man, how can you listen to a plan? Accept, examine, approve, reject a plan you may, but "listen" is not correct, though youth, with the oldest head on youngest shoulders, "I thank thee for the word." Who understands a plan so well as you, Johnny?

Why you're Shakespeare struck; this blessed tercentenary has turned your head—too much it's been for many of you.

No; not too much, wise-acre. If it but teach a tithe to read, mark, learn, and inwardly digest the works of him who wrought and wrote so lovingly and well.

Now listen I say, once for all, I can't get a word in edgeways. * * *

Well, that's new sensation anyhow for you, Master.

Banting says—

Ah! Banting

—"they call him—but a merrier man
Within the limit of becoming mirth,
I never spent an hour's talk withal;
His eye begets occasion for his wit;
For every object that the one doth catch,
The other turns to a mirth moving jest;
Which his fair tongue" * * *

Good gracious, "fair tongue!" how could such a Saxon be otherwise than fair? 'Tis indeed "love's labour lost" talking to you—but just hold your unfair tongue a moment.

What ho! punster, what ho! "Anon, anon, Sir!" "I pause for reply."

Now! Banting will meet us at Springfield with his trap; I shall be in Penrith, whither you must come by an early train, and after breakfast there * * *

Breakfast! "with what appetite we may." Oh! mind,

B

order trout with fried parsley, dos't hear? and insist on that
greasy and familiar waiter washing his hands and face for once,
by way of a treat.

Then we can post on afterwards. Now, are you game for
Whit Tuesday?

Certainly, if you'll only write to the weather office for a little
rain, and a change of wind—but seriously, send word to our
mutual friend as Podsnap has it, "ridiculous opportunity, but
so glad of it, I am sure." Bunting is a vasily agreeable
fellow; he remembers more than most men ever knew;
thoroughly understands what to eat, what to drink, and what
to avoid: and is of that remarkable class which is never in a
hurry, never late for a train, or behind an appointment; never
shocked nor surprised at whatever may turn up, nor perturbed
in the slightest degree by circumstances the most weighty and
perplexing. No one I should like to meet better, bar yourself,
of course—present company you know is always excepted in
personal allusions in good society; and as *Punch* tells us this
is sure to be a fine spring, as the year of grace 1864 is leap
year, we'll hope this cutting nor'-easter may change, and allow
us the hilarity of the charming season of hopeful spring in the
most delightful district of the north. Go? of course, old boy,
and in such company! I am so glad of the opportunity, I
really am.

Such was the invitation of my two friends on the 5th of May,
of whose genial hospitality I availed myself last August.

Happily, on the 11th, the wind veered round the right way,
and nothing could be more acceptable. Vegetation sprang
into activity as if influenced by a forcing house, fine rain assisting, as the French have it.

17th May.—Having done a good hour's gardening between
five and six at home, and polished off a batch of letters, I took
the early train for Penrith. Whit-Tuesday, in places where
the market is held on Mondays, is always, if the weather be
tolerable, the best holiday the hard-worked have. The morning
was misty, but of that kind indicating the approach of great
heat, and it was "most jolly" to see the happy faces of friends
and those to whom one nods, anticipating perhaps as much
pleasure as myself, whether they had it or not. All the way
from umbrageous Piercebridge, along that line by sunny Winston
and charming Selaby, up to blowy Barnardcastle, along the tortuous, leafy, sparkling Tees the route is lovely, and never more
so than on this day. From the airy structure of the ingenious
Bouch which spans Deepdale, one could see right and left, up
and down that charming ravine so famed for ferns and foliage,
the mist sweeping off, now revealing, anon concealing the view
so exquisite, in that manner peculiar to the summit of high
mountains. Arrived at the crest of Stainmoor, the vast plateau
of pastoral Westmoreland lies open like a huge map. The
variety of tint was brilliant in the now perfect sunlight, and a
sycamore, as if suddenly awakened into life ere its unfolded
leaves had deepened into green, shone as molten gold. Such
an effect I had never witnessed before, though three other
instances met our gaze in Newlands the following day. Though
the gradients are desperate, entailing a serious expenditure of

costly power, the railway with its stupendous viaducts, that over the Beelah being the highest in England, and flue bridges, is worth a journey of itself, and few points are more telling than the first peep of Kirby Stephen, the noted residence of Poet Close, and the important High Sheriff of the county. One of those extraordinary gatherings called a statute fair—against which as an institution so much just indignation some time ago arose, but which, like other spasmodic emotions of us English, has been a nine days' wonder and little more —was being held at Penrith. That small town, by its long enjoyment of railway communication, has distanced in influence all rivals, and become, with its seven means of access other than by rail, the centre of a wealthy agricultural district. Special trains, besides the ordinary traffic, conveyed many hundreds on business and on pleasure bent. "Punctual to his word," as he always is, my friend tarried for my arrival at the station, the train being just thirty minutes after time. But mark the crowd! Such Bœotians I never looked at. Though the special had cleared off vast numbers before our regular train arrived, we picked them up all along the line, station after station from Kirby Stephen, *Passau*, the gloomy valleys of Switzerland or Savoy could scarcely furnish forth a physiognomy lower in both sexes, the exceptional talent being nothing higher than low cunning. There were very few old people—I counted four—and all appeared to belong to the agricultural class—farm servants going to be hired at the statute fair, of which there are two every year, one in May the other in December. In elbowing our way, as best we could, through the densely crammed station, it was odd to observe piles on piles of huge boxes, large chests indeed, big enough to hold their owners, belonging to servants changing places. From the top of the 'bus the sight was strange ; all down the heart of the little town, nay to the very outskirts, was one sweltering mass of struggling human beings of the same low type. At certain places more carts and gigs stood on their bottoms, the shafts pointed as if to receive cavalry, than I ever saw assembled in an area so small, shewing incontestably the purely agricultural population of the surrounding district. Whether it is from want of the means of education — from laxity of moral control— from the extraordinary system of courtship adopted with the acquiescence of the girls' mothers — the apathy of those by whose hands discipline should be enforced—from climate—owing to a sparsely scattered population shut out from the world in most part, and without healthy amusements, or what not, through out Cumberland, so far as my own observation went, and particularly at this fair, the type of the people was the lowest—faces the weakest, heads the most animal I ever saw—and their manners, without meaning to be uncivil, perhaps the most uncouth : in fact an aggregate of healthy savages. While the neighbouring county of Durham shows an increase of 30 per cent in the population, as proved, by the census returns of 1861, during the interval of the ten previous years, Cumberland by the same table has but 5. Although Durham contains a mixed population of miners and mechanics, hard-fisted labourers of all kinds, in the year 1860 the illegitimate births in that county were only 5·4 per cent, yet in Cumberland the return is no less

than 12·1, or over 1 in 8 as against London, which is about 1
in 24 ! At these statute fairs, which occur throughout the
principal towns in the county, the orgies commence at three
o'clock in the afternoon in the open streets, and statistical
returns of the irregular births in wedlock, besides the state-
ment quoted, the causes of death, the amount of drunken-
ness, and the exaggerated number of cases of delirium tremens,
even in women, would be something appalling to Dean Close
and his clique, who want to make folks moral by Act of Parliament—"rob the poor man of his beer"—"starve out the
publicans"—and oust the education of the drama for the in-
flation of the platform. The people were in rude health ; I did
not see a single person pitted by small-pox, and only one
cripple. By far the quaintest of the motley crew was Lord
Brougham's steward. If he has any other name than this
honourable title, we could not make it out, so ignorant were
those from whom such information would invariably be gleaned
elsewhere, and of such "a character" too ! What a *carte* the
curious old bird, donkey chaise, and all away together, would
make, including the leather breeches !

Ballads are always instructive upon the interesting question
of the manners and customs of a people, and those pursuing
such inquiries as may here be excited are referred to Anderson's
collection of Cumberland ballads, wherein may be found his
note ill., p. 202, to

" When aw t'auld fwok were liggin asleep,"*

which appears to me—combined with the marked absence of
decent accommodation too frequent in farm houses—to be the
key to the whole mystery. It would be unfair to Cumbrians
omitting the fact, that, notwithstanding the crass ignorance and
extreme irregularity of their peasantry, the county shews a
sheet cleaner of heinous crime than most, and in that respect
will hold her own against all comers, as the following comparative analysis proves :—

STATISTICS OF CRIME (1860).

	Population, 1861.	Against the person.	Property, with violence.	Property, with-out violence.	Malicious offences against property.	Forgery and cur-rency offences.	Other offences.	Total.
Cumberland	205,276	17	7	56	1	1	—	82
Bedford....	135,287	2	6	58	3	1	1	71
Berks......	176,250	12	2	109	6	3	—	132
Bucks	167,993	13	8	81	1	4	2	109
Cambridge..	176,016	17	4	67	3	2	5	98
Dorset	188,789	24	7	106	1	1	7	146
Hereford ..	123,712	14	8	56	—	2	3	83
Hertford ..	173,280	4	6	79	8	3	4	104
Oxford ..	170,944	10	4	80	2	3	6	105
Westm'land.	60,817	3	1	15	0	1	—	20

Allowance must be made, of course, for excess of population.

* See Appendix.

After breakfast, my friend having some business to transact an hour was left me to stroll about, and among other sights I recognised, adorning an itinerant photographic establishment, the portraits of South Durham worthies, who would have been mightily chagrined, I trow, at being held so cheap. At one o'clock we posted to Springfield to join Banting. The day was deliciously hot, and the country fragrant with fresh greenery. On nearing our destination, true enough there was his trim trap in waiting, and soon out he came to welcome us in the hearty but placid manner of his wont.

How *are* you ? How are *you* ? *How* are you ?

Where do you *live* ? Where do *you* live ? *Where* do you live ?

(All three speaking at once, the trio adding.)

Very glad indeed. *Very* glad indeed. Very glad *indeed*.

Such the greeting, so English and so odd. We always call him "Banting," he's in such a funk at becoming corpulent and losing his figure, poor fellow—but he's a rare sort when you know him, though he has dropt his beer and taken to biscuits. He was just like a new pin—almost painfully neat—in short,

"The glass of fashion and the mould of form."

Most fortunately at this place, where the Patterdale station will be—the distance from point to point being nine miles—we were introduced to Mr G. Grant Boulton, the eminent contractor of the new line he expects to open in July, and by which Penrith will be immediately connected with Keswick and Cockermouth, thus making a direct and unbroken route by the North-Western and North-Eastern systems to Workington and Whitehaven, and in fact to all parts of the kingdom. Besides the immense advantage of passenger traffic to the Lake district, the superior coke of South Durham will be exchanged for the hematite of West Cumberland ; not only that, but the mountains which have for countless ages been a perennial beauty and delight to the eye, will yield, if we mistake not, an inexhaustible source of profit to man. Hitherto their boundless wealth has been sealed up for want of the very means of access now about to be supplied. That gifted woman Harriet Martineau, some time ago looked upon railroads in Westmoreland and Cumberland as the chimeras of enthusiasts. The venerable first railway solicitor when he prophesied, in the dawn of railway enterprise, that the locomotive would travel 20 miles an hour instead of the eight old George Stephenson was compelled to admit before the committee, was looked upon as distraught ; but once fairly in working order Mr Boulton's line is merely the harbinger of a complete system throughout the district, and not many years will pass over before Windermere and Derwentwater are linked together by iron lines, Ullswater having the benefit of a short branch to Penrith. The minerals in the neighbourhood of Keswick comprise a list so vast, of a value so immense, and a supply so bountiful, that the intelligence and the wealth which unquestionably will be brought to bear for their development must raise the character of the county from its present degradation. The contractor, in the most courteous manner, offered to take us by his little engine along a portion of the line, and the trap having been sent thither, sometimes driving, sometimes walking, we reached Mosedale, where one of the finest viaducts is built. The district abounds in beautiful porphyry and building stone in great variety and of the best quality ; of such materials then is the masonry constructed, and the colour of the works in such scenery is peculiarly harmonious. Although in the valleys the day was sultry, the air along that part of the line which traverses the Hutton Moor to Threlkeld was fresh and crisp—nothing could be more exhilarating. Retaking the trap, after thanking Mr Boulton, we drove down into Keswick, the approach to which is, every yard of it, more and more bewitching. Such a spring as this had not been known almost in the memory of man. The modest primrose sparkled in company with luscious whins and golden broom, lilacs, and laburnums, bird-cherry, horse-chesnuts, apple blossoms, campions, wood-roof, hair-bells, bird's-eye, cranes-bills, stellaria minor and major, wood-anemones, forget-me-nots, rhododendrons, azalias, hawthorn (red and white), herb-robert, crosswort, pimpernel, barberries, orchids, and ferns unfolding their graceful fronds to the summer sun in May. Dotted about here and there were seats of the gentry, their grounds and the whole country being ablaze with gorgeous colour, toned down with the freshest green of every shade, mingled with the early maroon of the sombre purple beech. No scene could be more delightful, but it was only an earnest of brighter gems in store. I have revelled in the luxury of Spring in the South of France, and the sudden splendour of Northern Italy, where Summer treads on Winter's heels, and this was as enchanting, nature seemed so buoyant and so tuneful, the very birds warbling new notes. As Banting was unable to put us up, apartments were ready for us at the George, where we dressed before his dinner at 7.30. About 9.30 some one " called for a calendar, and found it was moonlight to-night," so out we sallied to puff our " weeds" upon the lake, awakening the merry echoes with catches, questions, *Kooi Kooi* and *ranz des vaches* till nearly midnight. Such was our first pleasant day.

May 18th.—It almost escaped me to mention my disgust on finding there was no trout for dinner—Banting said it was foolish destroying a fine appetite by vexation, he was inured to every vexation ; at Keswick there was no such precaution, but at Lodore they have a tank always at command to prevent disappointment when fish wont bite—so to make assurance doubly sure, we found out a man of the name of Atkinson who promised everything ; first, that fish should be supplied for breakfast without fail this morning ; secondly, that he would accompany me before five a.m., for the purpose of catching it ; thirdly, that he would have his tackle and bait ready. In consequence, of course, I was out by 4.30, thinking it more prudent, having taken stock of him, to look after the man a little ahead of the time appointed. With the greatest difficulty, after belabouring his door and pitching gravel at his window, he was aroused out of a heavy sleep, and we reached the water's edge at 5.30 ; thus missing more than a good half-hour of another glorious morning. Atkinson is a man " when found to take a note on." He is a wonderful fellow to talk, and talks well. He told me that in July, 1846—it was awfully hot that year—he performed for the miserable sum of £10, more fool he, one of the most remarkable pedestrian feats on record, winning his wager with 19 minutes in hand. No man knows the country better, which is a grand point. Starting from home at seven p.m., he sped to and ascended Scawfell Pike, the highest English mountain, its altitude being 3,166 feet ; then he reached the base and attained the summit of Helvellyn, which rises 3,055 feet, and coming round by Skiddaw climbed that great mountain, no less than 3,022 feet high, by way of a finish ; and returned home smiling at 6·41 the following evening, the distance being between 70 and 80 miles, and the ascents and descents something perfectly astonishing, within his limit of 24 hours. He must have been in rare hard condition, as he lost only 3lbs. weight, and was hearty enough to enjoy the society of his friends immediately afterwards ; to whose home he had to travel an extra distance. The account of this performance is recorded in *Bell's Life*. The approach to equality in the various altitudes in the lake district is remarkable. The three mountains named are not far off each other in height. Fairfield is 2,950 feet, Great Gable 2,925, Saddle Back 2,787, Grassmoor 2,756, Red Pike 2,750, High Street 2,700, Grisedale Pike 2 680, Old-man 2,577, and Kirkstone Pass 1,200. Does this affect the argument of subsidence against eruption, as the cause of the irregularity of the earth's crust ? In 1851 I was present at a private gathering of *savans* at the house of an Italian friend, when Professor Belli, of Bologna, showed us the result of an interesting experiment, illustrative of the latter theory. He was the most speechless and reserved person I ever met out of an institution for the deaf and dumb, but there was a deal in him. As to his ingredients, he preserved a profound secrecy ; they were mixed in another room by himself alone. He then shewed us his liquid in a pan, and boiled it before our eyes. When cooked, he allowed us to see it cool, and in that process, sure enough, instead of subsiding, up gradually arose undulations on the surface representing, as he said, mountain-ranges, water-sheds, valleys, dales, and so forth. When cold the substance was as hard as metal, basaltic looking stone, and when fractured displayed curious stratifications, and line upon line in places like flints in the chalk formation. We asked no end of questions, but the oracle was dumb. Now the depth of the lakes is much more varied, Windermere being 240 feet, Ullswater 210, Bassenthwaite 68, Derwentwater 72, Crummock 132, and so on.

But to return to old Atkinson, who had as usual forgotten all about me and my fishing, trolling, and minnows, so the next best thing to be done was to set a lot of trimmers with live perch, in the hope of good luck, of which unhappily there was none, as we did not touch a fin, bar those of the unlucky bait, which were lively for hours. Nevertheless, the morning being so fine, mere existence was luxury, and it was impossible to feel annoyed, the man was so sorry and so civil. Marshall's island, with all its beauteous varied leafiness, looked more inviting than ever, and as my guide knew the gardener, we went over the entire place, and among other specimens examined a tulip tree of extraordinary growth. Returning home for a bath at

ten, our party sat down to breakfast precisely at eleven ; and I
mention this fact merely to note what, as an old traveller, has
always appeared to me to be the best mode of dividing a
tourist's day in hot weather. Invariably be out at five, after a
good cold tub, including the ablution of the head ; work hard
till eleven or even twelve. If at all fatigued or over-heated,
repeat the tub tepid, and then sit down to a real breakfast, not
of the simple tea and toast kind, or bread and water, or even
porridge, but a regular meal, served hot and hot, such as they
gave us this morning at the George. The *menu* ran thus—
there was tea, as a matter of course ; it is refreshing, and the
English always like it. We started with young radishes and
watercresses ; fried trout, lamb cutlets with potato chips, and
poached eggs, were served separately on the table. Cold veal
pie (very well made), calves' head mould, cold tongue, and
potted trout being on the sideboard, with a bottle of cool
Vin de Grave, which was excellent. Such exactly was the repast, to which we did mighty execution. After it, we wrote
letters or read newspapers or chatted till one. Then the horses
were ordered out, and we rode at an easy rapid walk by Portinscale, round the head of Derwentwater, through Sir John Woodford's property, where admirable improvements in road-making
are being carried out ; by Keskadale, whence, looking back on
Keswick, the lake, representing the Arno or the Inn, one is
forcibly reminded of Florence or Inspruck ; and so on right
up the steep road to the summit of Newlands Haws before
dropping down upon Buttermere. Even had the way been
less precipitous, the heat was too great to have gone faster than
a walk, which pace the nags did smartly, and the day was as
enjoyable in such weather and such scenery as is conceivable. We
were accompanied by a Scotch gentleman of the name of Wood,
the engineer of the new line, who to his many other accom-
plishments is a clever draughtsman. Just before halting, the
Honister Pass, Buttermere and Crummock water came in view.
Buttermere is small, only one and a quarter miles by a little
more than half-a-mile, and a plain sheet of water full of delicious char, which lie in deep places and are not yet in season,
at least we could not procure any for love or money. From
Crummock the rocks rise perpendicularly, and the whole scene,
bathed in the finest sunlight, was never witnessed in greater
perfection, much of the water being blue like Geneva. Usually
it rains hard there, and we might have gone twenty times without anything like such weather. There is only one miserable
sinffy little inn at the place, and a more wretched little church,
with an unfortunate parson, they told us, existing on a stipend
of £40 a year, and blessed, as Dean Swift sometimes was, with a
congregation consisting of the clerk and himself. With some
little difficulty and after a long delay—so strangely awkward
and queer the people, who are wondrously ignorant of all about
them- -we got a boat and rowed up Crummock water till we
neared Scale Force, having a little sport by the way. The
trout were in capital order, but being unable to carry them on
horseback they were given to the boatman. The Cascade is
the highest in the district. Owing to the dearth of rain,
there was very little water, and the attenuated stream fell
plumb 156 feet, like a long, delicate ostrich feather ; the big

walls of the chasm on either side of it were beautiful and fresh with rowans, hollies, hawthorn, wild flowers, ferns, oxalis, cedums, and lichens, dispersed in the most charming and fantastic manner possible. Of this waterfall our Scotch companion rapidly made a clever sketch. While waiting at the inn a carriage and pair drove up in almost wedding haste. The party consisted of four men and a youth. Each adult wore a veil round his hat, as if bound for the Derby at least, though there was little dust on that rocky road ; each was furnished with a bran new leather case about a cubic foot in size, and each shouldered a marvellous bundle of clean wood. They tumbled themselves out of the vehicle in a surprising style. Banting was diverted with the struggles undergone in the process of unknotting their legs and sticks, and we were all curious to make out what on earth they could be or might do first. One said, " Good heavens they're all cripples, look at their crutches !"—another, on seeing them get upon their legs, "No they are surgeons, there are the medicine chests and splints. Misery, an accident ! where—where ?" Then they began squeaking and squirting as only Yankees can talk and spit, so that settled their nationality at once. In they rushed, higgledy piggledy, all first and none last, to order tea with ham and eggs, and off again. Such the introduction. With as much activity, the boy re-reading a letter from his troubled home, the men were at various points photographing like mad, thus explaining their odd belongings. When we took horse to return, tea and ham and eggs, Yankees and apparatuses had all skedaddled, which hurried way of doing scenery amused Banting amazingly. Whether our steeds had had an extra measure, or were glad to get away—whether the varlets, who stood bye enjoying the joke, had gingered the brutes, or they were severally and respectively possessed with a devil, it is out of my power to determine : but on starting each beast behaved unaccountably ; in short, in the most outrageously cocktail manner possible. My cob, usually steady as a haystack, quite forgot himself. At first he ridiculously refused to let me mount at all, and even after yielding nothing could be more absurd than the snorts or " sneers," as a horsey authority has it, with which he executed a *pas seul* between a minuet and a hornpipe. The Scotchman and Master John, both well mounted with hands down, were off in a trice, and the playful kittens went tearing up the stony mountain road at a frightful pace. Banting was last out ; his gloves required buttoning, of course, and his cigar was only just alight. His slashing mare, with her rakish shoulders, deep chest, rare back ribs, powerful arms and thighs, lean head, and wiry neck, stotted, bounded, and curvetted in the most insane way. He was in the saddle, certainly, but there was no time for stirrups, and, alas ! his hat was jerked off, which spoilt the picture—but for that, no one would have known the whole affair was not intended and well done, so admirably did he sit at home at ease. Properly we should have returned by the Honister Pass and Borrowdale, but the distance would then have been increased by three miles, and our dislike to rapid travelling in such heat, amidst such beauty, combined with Banting's objection to being hurried or late for dinner, turned the scale in favour of

c

retracing our steps exactly. It is difficult to decide which is
the finer route, the journey or the return — but it is well to lin-
ger over both ways through Newlands. At first, if we had a
summer sunlight, we were afterwards, if possible, more charmed
with the warm flood of golden evening, and the shadows, in
one place like a great bear's skull, while at the head of Crummock, a ridge on the mountain side, another shadow, with
the outline of the rock assisting, curiously resembled a brace
of setters standing at dead point. It was just about half-
way in this delightful ride we observed the yellow sycamores
mentioned yesterday, like that on Stainmoor. Had they
been painted, folks would have thought them unnatural —
indeed, only Alfred Hunt, Brett, or young John Linnell dared
essay their vivid light, in any landscape. We arrived at the
George punctually at eight, the time appointed, allowing us
lots of leisure for tub and toilet, before 8·30 sharp, when dinner was served. Like all the good hotels in the lake district,
and they abound, this preserves a character for scrupulous
cleanliness. The linen, the plate, and the glass were unexceptionable in all respects. Situated in a street, it is shut out
from all view of the lake by Mrs Dewar's boarding-house, the
respectable head of which establishment is always keenly on
the look-out for the "Exquisite coach," and never so radiant
as when that vehicle is clustered with tourists. The George,
however, has the advantage of her garden, for from our windows we looked down upon lilacs and laburnums in full bloom.
Of course, Banting had ordered dinner ; it is quite a treat to
see him calmly go through that necessary and pleasing duty.
"To study where he well may dine," he strictly observes as a
species of devotional morning exercise. All I stipulated for was
trout, which came from Windermere, fried parsley, cucumber
cut in junks, not in thin slices, a boiled leg of lamb, with acid
rhubarb sauce, and plenty of new potatoes. The repast was
perfect ; each dish with its accessories being admirably served
individually, and dressed without a fault. All the wine, too,
was good and cool, while nothing could be more delicious than
the water from Skiddaw. At Portinscale, at the foot, and at
Lodore, at the head of the lake, are large hotels. In Keswick
itself also there is quite a group of them, but I doubt whether
there is to be found a hostelry so liberally purveyed as, or
better managed than, that we enjoyed. The house is kept by a
widow, Mrs Beethom, who with her daughters see personally,
without forwardness or fuss, to the comfort of everybody.
They thoroughly understand their work, the eldest daughter,
though quite young, being an unusually clever woman of business ; indeed, she is the lubricating oil of the whole machinery,
and I can heartily recommend the establishment in every way.
Now this was a toughish day, and another pleasant one.
Having left the subject short, let me say those requiring it may
take a cup of chocolate or coffee with a biscuit on rising, at
4·40 ; but I maintain that in travelling a man best divides the
day by starting work at five, continuing till at least eleven,
breakfasting and resting till near two, then again at work till
eight or nine o'clock, dining at half after ; bed at eleven, or
half an hour later, and a bath before each meal, not forgetting
Banting's injunction to sponge the head well as soon as you get

up ; he says it takes the cobwebs out of one's brains—and he's not far wrong. By this means the intensity and inconvenience of heat are avoided, one is never fagged, and the finest lights are secured. If you walk, of course, always soap your socks. Between 4 and 5 p.m. a glass of absinthe—of which invigorating liqueur the Messrs Plews, of Darlington, supply the best—or a cup of good tea, may be desirable.

19th May.—Yesterday we arranged with Atkinson to have an early fishing excursion upon what he called "an out-and-out grand scale." Of course, he promised everything, and to guarantee success would "engage a noted sportsman," named Bowe, I think, "who never failed, and provide 180 trimmers at least!" The man might just as well have said 365 when he was at it, but perhaps he wished to be moderate. However, after a ticket from the Vale of Derwentwater angling company had been obtained, for which the charge was the moderate sum of 1s, we changed our minds, not liking the trouble of being down by "5 a.m. at latest," with the probability of disappointment similar to my own ; it was far better as it turned out, for we were all three a little fagged with the unusual heat, and one was amiss. I am ashamed to confess that nine o'clock found me in bed, though the morning was just as glorious as yesterday's. Our mutual friend, with the old head on young shoulders, alas ! was suffering the excruciating disturbance a wisdom tooth often occasions. His illness threw a damper over us, so Banting and myself waited upon the doctor and called him in. He was a very intelligent, pleasant, and even common-sense man, too, though in that condition of extravagant bliss which is said immediately to precede matrimony. "Going to be married, are you ?" we said. "Lucky birds—we'll chalk you out a tour." Banting then became as excited as his idiosyncrasy would permit ; but, ever ready to make happy people happier, and dull ones too, he observed, referring in the most impertinent way to me, "Drybones ! will help us, I know. Where's your Bradshaw ?" so at it we went, chapter and verse, for 16 days in and out of London. The hotels were all spotted, and what to see in Paris, Bâsle, Lucerne, Strasbourg, Cologne, Brussels, and Antwerp, &c., and, of course, how long to remain in each place. At two o'clock, our patient being somewhat recovered, we were on horseback, and passing the house in which Southey lived, and the mother church, his honoured resting place, we marched through rich valleys, nestled among beautiful mountain ranges, by the blue and placid waters of sunny Bassenthwaite calmly sleeping at the base of big Skiddaw, bound for Peel Wyke, where the bog myrtle casts its spicy fragrance on the air. The wise tooth having become intolerable, we left its unfortunate owner to rest at "The Swan with Two Necks," where that quaintly comfortable specimen of humanity and kindness, the landlady, whom we called after her own sign, tho' unlike a swan of any variety conceivable, earnestly recommended a poultice made of porridge ! "Alas, poor Yorick !" The new railway to Cockermouth follows in great measure the old road a distance of 15 miles, and the line running by the very edge of Bassenthwaite, presents another most beautiful avenue to Keswick. Banting and I enjoyed the little ride to Peel Wyke much. He is great at wild flowers and ferns, with which the woods and banks abound ; happily for me he is not so well up in trees and horticulture, so there " I had him on the hip." But nothing is pleasanter than an agreeable chatty companion, full of information, ready alike to impart and receive it. This neighbourhood, though they say the variety of flowers is not so great as in that around Windermere, yet, I think it richer in ferns. Above one of the bays of Derwentwater, upon Sir John Woodford's property near Portinscale, the osmunda regalis flourishes almost as luxuriantly as near Killarney, and attains really a prodigious growth. In Borrowdale, the aplenium septentrionale is found, and very rare indeed it is. The silvery ceterach officinarum, the bortrychium lunaria, the ophioglossum vulgatum, ruta muraria, blechnum boreale, lastrea rigida, polypodies, and phegopteris are common about Keswick and the base of Skiddaw. In several places, but particularly yesterday in ascending Newlands, we found the parsley fern almost by the acre, and the oak fern, with its lovely green and hair-like stem, was in cushions here and there. Purple-stalked lady ferns, the sporting filix mas, indeed almost endless varieties of these interesting plants with awkward names, abounded ; but there were very few scolopendriums of any kind, at least so far as I saw, though the vulgare is reported common. Among so many rarer specimens, it was odd to miss so very ordinary a species, and as strange not to find many polystichums. The common spleenwort (asplenium trichomanes) flourishes at Ambleside ; the adiantum nigrum, at Ullswater ; the Cystopteris fragilis, near Ara force ; the Woodsia ilvensis, near Bowness ; the Lastrea oreopteris, at Fairfield ; the Polypodium calcareum, at Kendall Fells ; the Asplenium viride, on Scout Scar ; the Hymenophyllum Wilsoni, near Lodore and Scale force ; Lycopods at Kirkston, Great Gable, Ennerdale, Wastwater, Bowfell, Langdale, Skiddaw, and Helvellyn. Banting knew them all, and so did old Atkinson, who supplies them when written to, at least when he does not forget, which will be nine times out of ten. But the jolliest thing would be to hunt in couples for them ourselves, for which we had no time this journey. At Peel Wyke there will be a station and an hotel, the latter erected after the design, in Baronial Scotch, of Mr Ross, of Darlington, on Sir Henry Vane's property, which, like many others in these parts, will be materially enhanced by the opening of railway communication. This place will turn out one of the most favourite fishing quarters with which to start an angling tour. The lake always affords good sport, and there are undeniable trout streams within easy distance. At length we returned to "Old Mother Goose," picked up Master Yorick, much recovered by his rest, and quietly walked home for dinner at the George, which was as perfectly arranged as that of yesterday. Our mutual friend was still obliged, as he said, "to hold his jaw," poor fellow, much to our loss, for what with "his gibes and gambols, his songs and flashes of merriment, he is wont to set the table in a roar."

The clever young mistress of the house called the puddings on both days " Windermere ;" but I recollect five and thirty years ago bringing the receipt for precisely the same dish from Cumberland, under the name of "Castle," and few things of the kind are better. This is it:—Equal weights of eggs in the shell, flour and white sugar, with half the quantity of butter, put into cups and baked in a quick oven. They should turn out of a delicate fawn colour. They are like hot little sponge cakes, and are excellent eaten cold, with a good custard for those who like it. Ours were served with sugared melted butter, and a dash of cognac in it. A table-spoonful of fine old rum is what the Germans would adopt, and they are great at sweets. But the best sauce I know is clear arrowroot, with a wine-glassful of orange brandy. Don't know how it is made? Well! now 'tis beyond the season; but when Easter comes round again, don't forget to put the very thin peel of eight Seville oranges and eight plump lemons, a gallon of the finest new pale cognac, with 3lbs of the best white sugar, into a covered jar. Stir the mixture thoroughly twice a-day for three successive days, then strain and bottle it into white glass bottles, and let them stand on end some time. Strain off the clear liqueur, and don't allow the smallest sediment to mix with it—mind take heed of that. Let the sediment remaining from each bottle be put together, and after it has well settled strain off the clear liqueur again, bottle, and hermetically seal the corks. The remainder will do for the shooting flask. The peel is useful for culinary purposes when dried ; the pulp makes good marmalade, and the liqueur itself improves with age. In two years even, it is far better than most sorts one buys ; and after blackpuddings or ice is as fine as curaçoa sec at 10s a-bottle. And you don't know how to make English chutney? Really, I am so glad of the opportunity, I am sure. Take 1lb brown sugar, ¼lb bruised ginger (fresh if you can get it), ¼lb of garlic, the same quantity of ordinary onions, sliced and pounded fine, ⅛lb of mustard seed--toasted before the fire, but not bruised, mind that—½lb of raisins—stoned and chopped very fine, though Sultanas are perhaps better in every way and less trouble, as they may be used whole—½oz. of cayenne, 3 pints of white vinegar—that made from hock grapes, or white currants is the best. 15 sour apples, peeled and cored, must be well simmered in the vinegar and thoroughly bruised. When cold, put in all the other ingredients, and mix them together. Now, I am never without this pickle, for which if made at this season substitute green grapes or gooseberries for the apples. She was so agreeable and ready to take in and profit by hints in cookery that we got on famously. It was happily unlike the too common talking to a dead wall on so important a subject. One great reason of our having servants absolutely ignorant of the most rudimentary culinary art is that their mistresses in far too many instances are unable to instruct them in manipulation. In Glasgow, when a young lady is engaged, she undergoes a regular tuition, from the simplest to the highest effort in the kitchen. Now, listen a moment ; here is a very economical, and at the same time most excellent, soup you ought always to have in stock. It should be almost colourless, and as clear as water. Take 7lb of the knee or hock of beef, the bone sawn into three ; add 4 quarts of water, skim well on boiling, then add 2 carrots, 2 turnips (if you like them—or 2 Jerusalem artichokes), 2 sticks, or a pinch of the seed, of celery, 4 onions,

and a bunch of herbs — any kinds and all sorts you have.
In a muslin bag put 12 pepper corns, 6 cloves, and 2 blades
of mace. Then simmer the whole together for four hours,
strain frequently, putting the meat on a dish before serving ;
add as much of it (the meat) as you like, but observe the best
is the gristle and tendons next the joint. It is called Col.
Wood's turtle. We might have gone on for hours, Banting was
so attentive—

> Behold! his breakfasts shine with reputation ;
> His dinners are the wonder of the nation ;
> With these he treats both commoners and quality,
> Who praise, where 'er they go, his hospitality—

but we did not, tho' it was impossible resisting giving her a
receipt for orange jelly, which is so far superior to the opaque
kind one generally meets with. Pour upon an oz. and a half of
gelatine half a pint of cold water. Soak half an hour, then stir
in half a pint of boiling water until it is dissolved. Break
three-quarters of a pound of loaf sugar into lumps, and rub
them upon some of the rinds of the oranges and lemons to give
flavour. Squeeze the juice of twelve China oranges and four
lemons, strain off the pips of course, and mix with the
other ingredients in a sauce pan, stirring until the sugar is toler-
ably dissolved. Have ready three fresh eggs, well beaten with
the shells, stir them briskly into the jelly, after which be care-
ful not to stir them again. Put it on the fire and let it boil
five minutes. Then take it off, and allow it to stand two or
three minutes before passing it through the jelly bag. It
should turn out brilliantly clear. There now, young lady, and
all who haven't done so yet, try that, when fresh fruit come in.

Notwithstanding our invalid's condition he perked up wonderfully as the evening stole on, accepted a challenge from a
noted player, whose card was sent up, and won the rubber at
billiards in gallant style. There's pluck for you. The conversation after dinner was animated and interesting, turning
chiefly upon the early history of the County. Banting is a
sort of "book in breeches" for dates and derivations, having
ethnology and etymology equally at command. We had the
brave old Saxons talked over, who came from the district
betwixt the Elbe and the Rhine, and withstood the mighty
power of Charlemagne for two and thirty years, and whose
numbers in England never exceeded one million and a
half, notwithstanding their influence. The Danes too, God
help them now, to whose country, by the accidental wreck
of a vessel on the coast, the Lake District owes her breed
of hornless, hardy, little, grey-faced sheep called *Herdwick*,
which stand starvation better than any known species, and
when fat yield capital mutton. From the Danes we English
in a vast measure derive our love of truth, our indomitable
courage, our home affection, our enterprise on sea and land ;
while it is admitted our constitutional ideas of freedom and
representative Government, trial by jury, and other noble
kindred institutions, sprang from the deep root planted in our
grateful soil by the ancestry of those for whom our liveliest
sympathies are now more than ever excited. Their first incur-
sion is assumed to have taken place in 787, but their conquest,

or rather their motive of action, differed widely from that of the Saxons, who came to settle, inasmuch as it was undisguisedly to harry, and steal home with. Yet they stamped the people indelibly with their imperishable and invaluable character, while to this day no less than 60 per cent. of our language is directly derivable from their own—such their force. We went beyond these Norsemen and the Saxons to the ancient Britons, whom Bauting would persist in calling Kelts—we argued for Celts, but he was, as usual, inexorably proper; so Johnny 'woke up from his drowsiness with pain to ask if he went to Parry (Paris) last Easter. Now, there is much obscurity about these Celts, who migrated hither from the Continent at some dim prehistoric period, though they have left their names on almost every prominent natural object. Intrepid and warlike, their most powerful tribes were called Brigantes by the Romans, but Cymri or Cumbri by themselves, and hence the Saxon term Cumberland (i.e.), the land of the Kumbri. They occupied the whole territory extending from sea to sea, its southern limit commencing from the Mersey and the Humber, and extending northward to the district we call Northumberland and the lowlands of Scotland. The violent dissensions of their chiefs, tho' the last in the island to succumb, made them more than otherwise an easy prey to the Romans. The conquest of Britain by the Romans, commencing 55 B.C., was early interrupted, though Julius established a sort of Government ere his recall home, and England was left unmolested for an interval reaching to A.D. 43, when Claudius Cæsar completed the victory over a great part of the island, his army perpetrating atrocities unheard of. The final subjugation was accomplished, however, A.D. 80, when Agricola marched his legions by Mancunium (Manchester), along the western coast of Scotland, where he erected a chain of forts from the Frith of Forth to the Clyde, and then boldly pushing back through the conquered tribes four years later, he erected the celebrated chain of Stations from the Solway to Tynemouth, which were afterwards connected by an earthen rampart in the reign of Hadrian. The object of this great work was to check the Caledonians, who bade defiance to the Roman Eagle which swooped over our own kingdom till overmatched by them and the Saxons in 446. Nor did we forget the Bards and Druids, of whom the destroying host of Claudius made such hideous work, and whose mention sent Banting off to the piano and Norma. Their government was strictly that of a Priesthood, and therefore of irresponsible power; but oddly enough, they were upright and dispensed justice, not from any written code of settled law it is true, but on the immutable principles of equity. Their highest penalty was death, and their second excommunication, which was even more dreaded; but nothing could possibly be more solemn than their execution of criminals, the victims being immolated upon the very altars of their Temples, with every awful circumstance tending to impress and overawe the multitude. Their religious ceremonies were few, and idolatry was not practised by them. They adored the God of Nature without the trammels of superstition, or crafty dogmas elevated into essentials. Their principles were taught in public, and a moral life, in its strictest and its widest sense, they inculcated as the foundation of human wisdom and the source of human happiness. They eagerly studied medicine and the virtues of plants, the misletoe being their chief specific. To a man they opposed the Roman invasion, and hence by sheer weight to a man were they cut down. Great as engineers, they have left monnments of their skill almost as remarkable as those of the Egyptians. Stone circles in Cumberland and Westmoreland, of frequent occurrence as they are, must not, however, be attributed solely to the Druids, as there is good reason for believing that the majority of these curious rings were constructed by the Northmen. Ferguson fairly enough suggests, considering their constantly recurring visits, that they are relics of the *hœmegang,* a species of single combat, which, as its name implies, was originally held in a holme or island, but in inland situations a place artificially enclosed was substituted for convenience. Hence, also, Lord Ellesmere, in his "Guide to Northern Archæology," says it is supposed to account for the quadrangular enclosures found in Denmark and other Scandinavian countries. Tidemand,[*] whose admirable picture, "A Norwegian Duel," commands the admiration of all art-lovers in this year's Academy, has made these strange combats a peculiar study, and there may have been many a "duel of the girdle" practised in Arthur's Ring, near Penrith, that hard-bye Keswick, and other stone circles in the lake district, for aught we know, as the Danes then, as now, were the most obstinate devils to fight, and never knew when they were licked.

Then we got upon the subject of turnpike roads, which were established between 1750 and '60. To the present day throughout the district there are very few "gates" to pay, which is a monstrous comfort, and the horses and vehicles are unexceptionable. In 1752 the act was obtained for a road between Keighley to Kendal, and another from Heron Syke (where it joins the Lancaster road) to Eamont Bridge, near Brougham Post-chaises were introduced in 1754, carrier's waggons in 1757, and the first stage coach, drawn by six horses, and called "the Flying Machine," was seen in the county in 1763. The mail-coach passing through Carlisle and Kendal from Glasgow to Manchester, began to run 1786. In 1792 an act was passed for opening a canal from Kendal by way of Lancaster and Preston to join the Leeds and Liverpool canal; and in 1819 for another canal from Solway Frith to Carlisle. The Railway was opened to Carlisle 18th June, 1838, and in 1846 Penrith received that invaluable boon of modern civilisation. Our chat was so pleasant that Bantling and I had a struggle over just a single bottle of claret, which our younger friend said required to be seen to be believed; however, the night was so hot I could not face billiards, but stole away to bed before midnight, after another enjoyable day. The moon was radiant, but blaming the night expedition of Tuesday last for making the wise tooth angry, no suggestion of the "calendar," of course, was made.

May 20.—This morning was intensely hot; without an intervening cloud, the sun was positively scorching, and there was not a breath of wind to stir even an aspen leaf or the delicate foliage of the thorny acacia. Yesterday they said the glass stood at 84° in the shade, and the day previous but 2° lower ; what it was early to-day I never heard, but before eight a.m. it could not have been much under 90°, and the surface of the limpid lake, gleaming like polished glass, resembled the clearest oil. In passing over it one could see with the greatest ease the fish lying lazily at the bottom, or slowly moving in their transparent element, and the few weeds were beautiful. Having, almost in vain, tried to arouse snoring Atkinson, with whom I wished to have a pull upon the water, by mere accident a rook-shooting party overtook me, and being recognised by Mr Wood, was kindly asked to accompany them to Lord's Island, the largest on the Lake, once the seat of the Radcliffes, or Ratcliffes, and therefore interesting by association. I never beheld any effect in my life so delicious as the reflections. Marshall's Island was so accurately repeated, even to the most subtle tone and gradations of line, that had it been photographed from life the picture would have presented as much correctness on one side as the other—like Col. Stobart's gem of a Turner in the Bishop Auckland Polytechnic just closed. The wooded, gorsey hills on the other side produced the most charming bits of colour ; and I often wonder how it is that far-receding objects are thus represented at such a distance. At Vevey, for instance, the summit of Mont Blanc is reflected beneath, though it is miles and miles away. Oh ! there's nothing like early morning for clear light and air.

> " Magnificent
> The morning rose, in memorable pomp,
> Glorious as e'er I had beheld—in front
> The lake lay laughing at no distance ; around
> The solid mountains shone, bright as the clouds,
> Gorse-tinctured, drenched in empyrean light ;
> And in the meadows and the lower grounds,
> Was all the sweetness of a common dawn—
> Dews, vapours, and the melody of birds,
> And labourers going forth to till the fields."

The row was delightful ; the floating island had submerged since August, but St. Herbert's Isle, Ramp's Holme, Vicar's Isle, looked serene and lovely. Arrived at the rookery, we managed to make a fair bag of the inglorious game. Mr Wood's minié was a very handy weapon, once the property of a New Zealand chief. Finding I had never used a rifle, he kindly gave me five shots, the first brace of which struck an outer right and left, the second grazed each bird also right and left, while the fifth bullet hit the mark to a hair, which was pretty well for a novice. Returning towards breakfast-time, a very ominous and angry ripple came upon the lake with a chill. The wind had changed, a storm approached, not a fish rose, and clouds " at first no bigger than a man's hand," soon packed and massed themselves together, foretelling weather. In 1839, when that furious wind occurred so many will remember as devastating fine estates in this country and in Ireland, the effect on Derwentwater was singular. The fearful gusts reached the very bottom of the Lake, and blew bushels upon bushels of fish upon the shore ; even those varieties like char and vendace (a species of fresh water herring like those in Como) which lie in the deepest holes. Since then, char are unknown in it,

D

those left being pike, perch, and trout—none of them great weights. After breakfast it was arranged we should visit the station for Keswick, now in course of erection, and close bye the new hotel, also in progress. The well-selected site is on rising ground by the river Greta, at the foot of the Skiddaw, and in one of the finest amphitheatres of the district. The blinding dust whirled about, and the sky but lately so clear was completely overcast—there was more than a threatening of rain, yet we reached the spot, and returned to the hotel without a ducking. The station and the hotel are each built of Borrowdale slate, but the former has ordinary stone facings, while the latter presents the most admirable effect, owing to a beautiful rosy freestone from Lamenby, near Penrith, having been adopted by the tasteful architect, Mr Ross, whom we had the good fortune to meet on the spot. He was kind enough to show us his plans, and explain all their detail. No one better than this rising young man more thoroughly understands economical interior accommodation ; the elevation also of his work in hand does him infinite credit. By way of increasing the importance of the building its plinth is boldly bevelled, which produces a wonderful improvement upon the ordinary plumb line from the base. Whether the railway company will retain this hotel, for which it is said £500 a-year rental has been already offered, in their own hands or no, the course of events alone will solve ; and whether a select body of directors will start the little Saltburn games, and become commissioners ever ready to improve the occasion, time will shew. The sites of the two new railway victualling ventures, one at the extreme East, the other at the West of the Darlington Section, are almost equally perfect : but the conditions precedent are widely different. At the sea side everything is raw and untried, entailing therefore on the shareholders enormous annual loss, besides the outlay of dead capital to an amount that has never yet been admitted. At Keswick, however, there is an old point of attraction, a long established good will, to which the readier means of access will at the very outset give increased impetus, and such undoubtedly will be the rush of visitors that too much or too excellent accommodation can scarcely be provided. As yet the Zetland Hotel is useful only as a sort of educational establishment, in which directors and their special friends may be initiated into the mysteries of refined French cookery, and is scarcely resorted to by staying company, in consequence no doubt of the expensive charges, and an absolute dearth of diversion which a place requiring so much loose cash should afford. But, inasmuch as practically the same directory is at work in both places, it is to be hoped the shareholders' patience will not be pushed to extremity at both ends of the line, for notwithstanding individual advantage to the few may be secured at the expense of collective loss, there is a limit which prudence dictates. How venial soever it may be that railway companies should erect hotels as a commercial speculation in connection with their undertakings, it seems to the most casual observer extremely questionable policy in directors or any section of such a body becoming Licensed Victuallers personally or by deputy, quite independent of the question of the absurd inconsistency of such traffic on the part

of strict teetotallers and supporters of Mr Somes, as some are.
Let me not be understood to convey the idea that the Saltburn-
by-the-Sea charges, though high, are extravagant. If people
will indulge in *diners à la Russe* admirably served, with wine
as good as a man need wish to drink, of course they must put
money in their purse. What I mean to indicate is that such
an hotel as that erected in such a place, and managed as it is
by a committee, is not conducted in the way one would deal
with one's own speculations. For if any person incapable of
keeping a public was rash enough to make a similar venture he
would surely count the cost, and avoid a positive annual loss
of something little short of a handsome income if the truth was
told ; what the actual amount is I cannot make out from published accounts, and forbear all questions. We three have had
experience of these *diners à la Russe.* Not with directors and their favorites, mind ; but quiet little parties of
eight and ten. The Chêf, Mr Clift, is decidedly one of
the most accomplished artists of the day, and with so little
help as he had, with kitchen accommodation so ill and
ignorantly arranged, it is nothing short of marvellous that his
success was so complete as we found it on two occasions lately.
I have enjoyed the highest efforts of as many of the best cooks as
most fellows in my time and of my class, yet for sauce *Tartare*
—whitebait—*consommé de volaille aux points des aspergese—
pétites bouchées à la Sultana*—curry—iced gooseberry fool —
one of the very best things out at this season—*crême au
chocolât, and crême à la pistache*, commend me to the Zetland
Hotel—aye and pic-nics, honeymoons, afternoon or evening
entertainments of any description, if the guests are beyond the
capacity of one's own house or *service.* That, however,
is not the question at issue. It is a great point undoubtedly to be able to get what you are willing to pay for,
which nobody has had a chance of achieving in the North
at any hotel I know of equal to this. At Keswick a de-
mand will be supplied—at Saltburn the supply is demanded at
a positive and long-extended dead loss. The place will well
answer the anticipations and suit the book of the Improvement
Commissioners, who have bought land cheap and dispose of it
at a high price, as well as all who have building material in
stock ; but is the venture for the benefit of the shareholders, and as the Hotel is built, should it not be let
to an active, competent, and guaranteed person in the trade ?
" Shylock ! the world thinks, and I think so too," that the
whole thing is " a mistake," which Talleyrand said " was worse
than a crime."
We had much interesting conversation with Mr Ross and
Mr Boulton, who also happened to be at the station, upon
the minerals and the produce of the Lake district generally with
reference to the future development by the railway system.
The fine blue slate, of which the hotel was being constructed, is
yielded in almost inexhaustible supply from Borrowdale and the
Honister Pass, as well as from the Patterdale end of Ullswater.
At present, owing to cartage, it is very expensive, the price per
yard for roofing being something like 4s 3d, which so soon as
the line is opened will be reduced by at least one shilling, and
that will make a material difference per ton. Limestone is also

abundant. In some places it is burnt in large quantities, and sent into the West of Scotland, the produce at Alston alone in 1856 being 2,411 tons. Cumberland appears to have possessed manufactories at a very early period. There were fulling-mills at Cockermouth and Dearham in the reign of Henry III. A fustian manufactory was established in Carlisle in 1660, and one of broad cloth at Cockermouth about the same date. Some 30 years afterwards there were iron forges at Millom, and fulling-mills at Bassenthwaite where woollen cloths called "Skiddaw greys" were dressed. The cotton trade is located principally at Carlisle. A manufactory of coarse linen, sail-cloth, and such like at Whitehaven and other places. Paper is made extensively on several of the rivers; woollen fabrics at Keswick, as shewn by an ancient inscription on a flagstone—

" May God Almighty grant his aid
To Keswick and its woollen trade."

Earthenware, copperas, &c., at different points, while at Whitehaven, Workington, and Maryport there are several ship-building yards. The present Lord Lonsdale is constructing magnificent docks at Workington, and those at Whitehaven are by no means despicable. Formerly considerable salt-works existed at Bransted, Whitehaven, Netherall, Workington, and elsewhere in the county, and it is said the Romans worked an iron mine not far from Keswick. The plumbago or wad of Borrowdale, as the lead is called of which drawing pencils are made, is worked irregularly, and the price remains prohibitive, but now that so large a supply of graphite is coming from Sweden and Siberia at comparatively the most trifling cost, no increase of trade need be expected hereabouts from this hitherto exceptional mineral. Cobalt has been found in small quantities in Newlands, where we were on Wednesday, antimony at Bassenthwaite, lapis calaminaris, manganese, galena, and spars of various kinds throughout the neighbourhood. The yield of lead is very large, and will form a considerable item of mineral traffic. Alston is the principal site of the mines which are almost exclusively the property of the Commissioners of Greenwich Hospital, to whom they were granted by Act of Parliament on the attainder of the Earl of Derwentwater, whose possessions were immense in Cumberland, though neither they nor his influence saved his noble head in those dark and bloody times. In 1861, seventy nine lead mines in Cumberland and six in Westmorland yielded 6,324 and 2,392 tons respectfully, and the quantity of silver extracted from the former was 37,115 oz., as against the 39 mines in Northumberland and Durham yielding 19,536 tons and 78,261 oz. respectively. The quantity of ore yielded from the former counties in 1856 was 7,311 tons, containing 5,321 tons of pure lead and as much as 51,931 ounces of pure silver. They said both silver and copper are often found in some of the mines in the same veins as the lead ore. The principal mass of the carboniferous limestone and iron-producing districts in the northern counties emerges from beneath the coal measures of Northumberland and Durham on the East, and is bounded by a steep declivity commanding the valley of the Eden on the West. It reaches its culminating point on the long mountain range of Cross Fell, and forms the vast tract of moorland in the neighbourhood of Alston, about 425 miles in width ; and in the high and dreary region adjoining the Scottish border extends nearly from sea to sea. After an interval of some miles towards the West the same formation again rises from beneath the new red sandstone of Penrith, and the coal-measures of Workington and Whitehaven—lapping, so to speak, as a narrow belt or zone around the older slaty rocks of the lake district, which it almost entirely encircles. In the north, the actual limestone plays but a subordinate part,"and alternates with a grit-stone, shale, and other rubbish. A shaft suuk, for instance, near Cleator, shows as follows : —

	Ft.	in.
Dark shale	150	0
Coarse grit	36	0
Shale	30	0
Whirlstone	12	0
Shale	54	0
Red limestone	7	0
Shale	1	8
Hematite pierced to a depth of	32	0
	328	8

The hematite (red ore, sesqui-oxide of iron) from the neighbourhood of Whitehaven, is unquestionably the most valuable mineral, from which so much commerce is certain to flow from West to East, for the purpose of judicious blending with the leaner product there. It occurs in the carboniferous limestone, near the outcrop. The greater part of the excavations whence it is extracted are subterraneous, but at a place called Tod-holes, near Cleator, it rests so near the surface as to be worked by a simple open cutting. The floor of the deposit is a white and red mottled shale almost of the nature of fire-clay, and belongs to the limestone series. Bore-holes have been sunk in it to the depth of 30 or 40 feet without meeting with any other intervening material ! It varies in places from 15 feet in thickness, and is for the most part a dense mass of red ore, subdivided by irregular and nearly vertical joints. Small cavities rarely occur adjacent, when the ore assumes those botryoidal forms commonly called kidney, and the lumps or clustered nodules are certainly as like beast kidneys as they well can be. In such parts rock crystals are found, and calcareous spar and areogonite appear to be the last substances which have crystallized in the hollows. The ore almost invariably occurring in basins, it is doubtful whether it is a vein or bed. The quantity produced in 1856 was 267,256 tons, of which 8,089 were yielded from the Alston district, the rest being from that of Whitehaven. These quantities, however, must have been immensely increased since, owing to the facilities of transit obtained by way of Tebay, though in the year mentioned 51,470 tons were conveyed to Newcastle and Middlesbro' alone, and the total produce of pig iron in that year from the hematite furnaces of Lancashire and Cumberland was 25,530 tons. Millom produced 2,268 tons of iron pyrites which sold for £1,100, and contained 47 per cent. of sulphur. From the Alston mines 443 tons of barytes (carbonate) were obtained, and 378 tons of zinc valued at £1,400. The latest statistics we could find on the moment were in 1861, when Cumberland supplied 472,195 tons of ore, and 55,165 of pig iron as against 10,780, and 385,290 from Northumberland and Durham respectively. The seven copper mines in Cumberland and Lancashire raised 2,331 tons in the same year—in fact it is impossible to estimate the mineral wealth of the district, but by way of illustration we heard that only a few years ago a small estate was offered to one of the mining companies in the Western divison for £750. The purchase was declined, but they took the royalty, and have since paid the fortunate owner of the property as much as between three and four thousand a-year ; while the firm, consisting only of four, annually divide something like the same amount per head—so "it is an ill wind that blows nobody good."

From both Mr Ross and Mr Boulton we received the most patient attention to our many inquiries, and hence these figures, all having an important bearing upon the question of the investment of the railway, to complete which they have so much at heart. In 1861, the 28 collieries of Cumberland raised 1,255,644 tons as against the 271 of Northumberland and Durham, whence 19,144,965 were yielded. With such prospects of developing, as well as latent, wealth in combination with a neighbourhood of unrivalled attraction brought home to the east side of the island, no doubt whatever can rest upon the mind of the least hopeful that the Cockermouth, Penrith, and Keswick Railway is a venture with success assured. At the close of our conversation, Mr Boulton kindly shewed me his cabinet of minerals—and fine illustrative specimens indeed they were—found, as each was, in the district so soon to be opened out to the capitalist. The line is to be worked, so far as mineral traffic is concerned, by the Darlington section of the North-Eastern Company, while the North-Western take the passengers in hand. Such a duality revives the recollection of the death of the oldest and most prosperous railway company in the kingdom, while it deepens the feeling that, if merger and amalgamation, suicide or methodical madness as some say, were really necessary—which independent shareholders are as loth as ever to believe—a union with the North-Western, rather than the North-Eastern, was the obvious interest of all but the smallest minority.

There was no doubt whatever about the impending storm, and but for the inconvenience of a wetting before reaching the Hotel, where however we were housed dry, the rain clouds and sweeping distant showers added great effect to the beautiful scene from the site of the station. We had intended threading our way up the Greta, across which the new railway continually passes, and where by far the prettiest bits on the line will be, but that was now unfortunately out of the question. We thought, too, of visiting a little Methodist chapel, lately erected by Mr Ross, who has his hands full always here, which I had previously seen in the course of construction, and much admired ; but it was more prudent to postpone that pleasure. Banting's trap was counter-ordered, and we posted back to Penrith through a drenching rain, which no doubt benefited the thirsty land, although it came with an uncomfortable chill and aggravated the wise-tooth.

On the road, excited by the previous investigation, we were led to discuss the manufactories of the district, and found that in 1861 the comparative table ran thus :—

	No. of Factories.		No. of Spindles.		Powerlooms.		Total persons employed.
WOOLLEN.							
Cumberland	10	..	6,087	..	30	..	216
Westmoreland	9	..	17,724	..	84	..	492
Lancashire..........	101	..	227,655	..	6,377	..	9,227
Total of England and Wales	1,456	..	1,846,850	..	20,344	..	76,309
FLAX.							
Cumberland	9	..	27,442	..	9	..	1,325
Westmoreland	3	..	4,644	..	—	..	303
Lancashire..........	13	..	117,412	..	489	..	3,381
Total of England and Wales	136	..	344,308	..	2,160	..	20,305
COTTON.							
Cumberland	15	..	136,212	..	1,761	..	3,281
Lancashire	1,979	..	21,530,532	..	305,423	..	315,627
Total of England and Wales	2,715	..	28,352,125	..	363,125	..	407,598

Both Cumberland and Westmoreland are important agricultural counties. As in the dales of Yorkshire, there is a vast number of yeomanry, small 'statesmen, rich and independent, as well as intensely obstinate, tenacious, pugnacious and litigious—every man holding by his own, and coveting the possession of land with the utmost pertinacity. The country where eligible is cultivated, but where in Scotland, dotted upon the mountain slopes and over the high moorland, one would see flocks of sheep, the number was comparatively small indeed ; and as for game between Penrith and Keswick and back again we did not count a single head. We joked Mr Boulton by the bye about his navvies' partiality for poaching ; but he replied his were a very decent set of fellows to deal with, with whom hitherto he had had neither strike nor trouble, having invariably accommodated their wants by anticipation, and tact of course, and that high preserving was not the fashion in the neighbourhood. One cannot take leave of such a place as Keswick without recommending all interested in such sights to inspect Flintoft's model in relief of the district, than which nothing gives so rapid and so truthful an idea of the country, as well as the best means of traversing it. Crossthwaite's museum should be seen also. He who collected it and invented the life-boat and the æolian harp died in 1808, but his intelligent daughters survive to explain the collection. Then, there is a gallery of the native artists—the Pettitt's pictures, well worth a visit—and a first-rate lapidary, Mr Furness, to call upon. From Mr Wright, the botanist, geologist, and mineralogist of the district, who lives in the town, every information may be gleaned within the range of his special and extensive studies, his repeated interviews with the King of Saxony, Sir Roderick Murchison, Professor Sedgwick, and other scientific men who have appealed to him for local help, constitute him as the authority to be relied upon. Those anxious for an unrivalled view, should at sunrise, at sunset, or when the moon is up, by all means not neglect the Castle-head or hill. The place, close by the town, goes by each name, and on its summit the unfortunate Derwentwaters reared a castle, whence the Countess, at once the instigatrix and participatress of the Earl's rashness, his joys and sorrows ending in cruel fate, escaped when he was captured for being "out" in 1715, after securing the family jewels and valuables, only to be uselessly sacrificed in his behest. At the journey's end, our quarters in Penrith were spacious and beautifully clean, but the *cuisine* and all the wine, without exception, were sadly inferior to what they gave us at the George, and the cold was so intense the first thing was ordering the fire to be lighted. The storm was evidently electric, though there was neither thunder nor lightning in the neighbourhood, and the rain was partial, notwithstanding a furious burst raged in so many parts of England, creating great destruction of life and property in the North East of Scotland, North of Ireland, South of England, Lancashire, Cheshire, North and East Ridings of Yorkshire, and whole of the county of Durham.

May 21st.—After the rain and cold of yesterday this morning was bright, genial, and elastic, without the least oppressiveness in the 'atmosphere. We were about to suffer the loss of one of our party, for even had not business hastened his return, Yorick's constant suffering—poor fellow, he could not open his mouth to admit any thing beyond a teaspoon now—rendered home comforts imperative. Well, he left, and Banting, who is a *gourmet* to the back bone—choice almost to eccentricity in all his ways, his belongings, and his doings—said last night, "Now, this won't do, he's going, and two's almost as bad a number as one, for travelling; we must have a third, even if the fellow does naught but listen and approve, you know—yet he might throw in an idea now and then, perhaps, by mistake, and that's something. So I have asked "Tom Jones" to join us."

"Ah! pleasant company he ought to be, if there's anything in a name—with all my heart, though we could have hobbled on together better than most couples, and I had all the picking of your brains to myself, yet perhaps that would have been selfish."

"Ah! here he is," and we were introduced.

There's a picture of ruddy health for you, with as much intelligence as you'd see combined in a long day's march. Above the middle height, yet not tall—stout, broad, thickset and well put together—without an ounce of fat, or extra beef. Strong as a castle, and active as a kitten. Head well set upon the shoulders—ears small, and packed closely in—nose and mouth firm, without coarseness—hair crisp and fine, shewing the clear skin through it, but not thin—forehead broad and full, with the back of the head to match. Chin chiseled, hands and feet hard, clean made and not too small—step elastic, gait erect, action quick, without the slightest fuss. Complexion dark russet—eyes bright and penetrating, with a sweet expression, and a set of regular white teeth, sharp enough to bite a badger's tail off. Not know what's in a man when his hat's on! Why, sir, he would storm a fort, or woo a woman easily alike

—never turn a hair at the heaviest of small hours—match a turkey in digestion—and go through any amount of calculations, when others were dead beat. Such was our new companion, with whom I at once took a stroll through the little town, in search of stereographs, which we soon discovered, very well executed by a young artist of the name of Ogle. It would be too much to say his works equalled Wilson's, of Aberdeen ; Brown's, of Saltburn-by-the-Sea; Mudd's, of Manchester; or Piper's, of Ipswich, (whose prize specimens are perhaps the finest things yet produced,) but they are very mellow and happy for all that.

"Ah ! look there," as we crossed the market place, "that's a four-years-old Scotch wedder, or I'm a Dutchman."

"How on earth do you know ?" he said.

"Know ! observe the bloom on his back—that delicious dapple—the mulberry on his shoulders, and the deep tone of colour between his ribs —he has a full mouth for a crown. Butcher, turn up his head an' please you?—and so he has, of course. Cut me both legs off, if you can spare them ;" but what a flat I was not to secure the saddle too. Yorick said his was the best joint he ever ate, and I can answer for the other —and only 8d a lb. ; but it was the last of the Mohicans, for I tried since, at least both Banting and Jones did for me, but without success. What a wonderful little place Penrith is for chemists' shops ; there are four of them that would be no disgrace to London, and that is something extraordinary for a small provincial town of 7,189 inhabitants. But then the neighbourhood is crowded with gentry and well-to-do people, so that accounts for the anomaly. The county balls, at which "the quality sport their diamonds" to the wonder of little folks, are held in the hotel we were in, and the County Court as well ; as the boy Jones was interested in a case that day, we went in. Didn't the judge polish them off fast—not with Dowling dispatch, certainly, for he is *sui generis*, and I'll back his Honour to utter more wit—not always of the nicest either— and more law, as well as do more solid justice, than any other man, or any brace of them, in thrice the time.

Well, Yorick off with the mutton, and our carriage stopping the way at one p.m., we rattled off at score for Brougham Hall, where everything is in the best possible and most refined taste. The whole place is kept to perfection. The iron-work would enchant an antiquarian, and South Kensington might envy the door handles, the hinges, bell-pulls, knockers (one of which is the counterpart of that bird-like grinning demon at the main entrance of Durham Cathedral), the dogs and fire-irons, locks and bolts, which set me a thinking of Nuremberg, Florence, Venice, Genoa, and Milan. It is handsome, solidly handsome outside, and admirable in. The views from the windows are charming, and some of the timber is magnificent. The walnut-trees, for instance, equal those at Womersley, even those sacrificed by the hard winter of 1860. These shewed no trace of injury whatever. The ancient and perfectly restored chapel, too, is quite a gem of its kind, and outside of it the purple stemm'd and thornless rose was in a blaze of bloom — and very early it was. The rooms were all most comfortable ; and in the library, of irregular form, were several interest-

E

ing portraits, indicative and characteristic of the great original, their collector. Sterne was there, Elizabeth Cromwell, Sheridan, Burke, Rousseau, Dryden, Voltaire (a most capital picture), Fairfax, the Duke of Richmond, Humboldt, Francis I., and "though last not least in our esteem," Cromwell himself. But what I looked for most of all was Lord Brougham's mother—for such a child must perforce have had a great mother, as had Katharine Parr. And in the next apartment—a sort of ante-room—there the old lady sat in state. You might have spoken reverentially to her ; salute we did, thanking her for bearing such a son—the champion of the oppressed, matterless their colour or their clime, he who, thank God, still rivets the attention of the highest tribunal of the world for talent and for honour—enchains all hearers in the most erudite academies of science in this country or in France —charms by his writings, and fascinates by his tongue, alike gifted compeers, wittiest of women, or the most artless child. We saw over the whole house—every portion of it furnished with curious and consummate taste, his own study being perhaps the plainest, yet most interesting. Its walls were lined with portraits of contemporaries, chiefly French, and the place of honour was given, as well it might be, to Alexander Humboldt, in his room at Berlin, whose likeness was admirable, and to his daughter when a child, whose death caused such deep distress.

The day had changed, and the cold was all the more searching, owing to the sudden revulsion. Notwithstanding my back to the horses, I was so perished that enjoyment was out of the question, and ever and anon the neglected warning came uppermost—

"Ne'er cast a clout, till May be out ;"

rendered all the more impressive by the fact of having only summer clothing packed up, and Banting's buffalo robe left behind into the bargain. However, as good luck would have it, there was neither rain nor dust, and the nags soon set us down at Lowther Castle. Dear me ! what a time it is since first I saw it, though 1829 is not so far back after all. Then it struck my unaccustomed eyes as a wonderfully grand residence, and now, although it does not look a pin the worse for wear, the exterior seems much too regular for a style in which irregularity is most pleasing, while the rooms appear naked and unfurnished from want of colour—in fact, in inferior taste to Brougham. Erected after the designs of Sir Robert Smirke upon the ruins of the old hall, destroyed by fire in 1726, accounts have been discovered showing bills to the amount of £380,000, so that taking into consideration material supplied, independent of payments down, the cost must have been the thick end of half a million, and that's a lump of money. William, the present Peer, during the whole of his career, whether in the Lower or the Upper House, has deserved his high reputation as a first-rate man of business. No one looking at him, or listening to his sententious remarks, could fail being convinced of his talent, and perhaps a better Postmaster-General we never had. I have that opinion from those who worked with and under him, and no better judges can be. But as a large landed proprietor, as one understanding wealth, not for the advantages it brings

personally so much as the blessings it confers where properly
employed, he is conspicuous as a benefactor to his neighbourhood, and an honour to his class. Largely interested in various
public works, such as docks and mines, in the West, he has
done more to develope the trade and resources of his counties
than any other man past or present. None have been more
prominent in improving the public roads of the district, and as
a landlord his example is, and has been, of infinite value. Des-
pising, with the thorough contempt common-sense engenders, the
old system prevalent about him of feasting tenantry with a
week's gorge at Yule, and letting them dine with Duke Hum-
phrey till Christmas came again, he makes it a matter of business to provide daily labour during the whole twelve months,
so that no man is without work and wage. Thus he has con-
siderably raised the position of his people, and rejoices in
estates physically and socially the best managed in the neighbourhood, while as an agriculturist, practically grasping the
difficulties of farming—once considered "as easy as driving a
gig"—perhaps that's true, as it takes a clever fellow to do
either well—he makes tilling and breeding worth his while.
You have only to look at his cattle and stock generally, as well
as the condition of his property, to see this at a glance. As a
connoisseur of art, Lord Lowther, before he became the Earl of
Lonsdale, has long been known ; and anticipating a grateful
posterity he has with all the attributes of his career at his feet,
placed a life-sized marble statue of himself on the first landing
of the principal staircase of the Castle, right in front of the entrance. It is an odd idea certainly, and some might call it vanity,
but I can't discern the difference between such a work and a
picture one so often sees, or " when it was two guineas on ivory,
and you took your chance pretty much how you came out,"
excepting that of cost. As an example of art portraiture,
Stevens' statue is unexceptionable, and those who turn up
their little snubby noses at a man spending much over himself, including the horses, sheep, implements, and grain—
blue books on this subject and that, not forgetting the frag-
ment of art about the pedestal, but all fairly illustrative
of character, and curl their thin lips in disdain, let us
see what they, under circumstances similar, would have done.
Something in worse taste, I'll warrant, and not worth a tithe
of the value, let alone the outlay. His lordship has no gas-
works like those at Brougham, and how in the world the place
is thoroughly warmed I can't conceive. This day it was like
wandering amidst tombs, and very uncomfortable tombs too.
The rooms are well proportioned, but there is sad coldness in
the ceilings and the walls ; the pictures were excellent, particularly the Dutch ones, but with the exception of a
few—some glorious examples of Tenters—as good a Jan
Steen as exists—two Lawrences—the late Lady Lonsdale and
George IV. among others for instance—quite equal to Lady
Grey, Young Lambton, the lovely Howards, and Lord Eldon—
the choicest were all cabinet works. Wouvermans, Ostade, Breu-
ghel (volvet), Gerard Dow, Vanderwerf and Vandervelde belng
amongst them, and a clever little Murillo ; but it was so abomi-
nably cold I could not enjoy them half enough. Fanatics talk
about their devotions keeping them warm in a damp church ;

If that be true, the sooner some of us are devotees the more enjoyment we should have ; though as at present advised, I don't believe such nonsense as the mind being at command at all when the body is ill at ease. The gems in this collection are not alone confined to the painter's art, as the antique marbles are worth much more examination than our time or the atmosphere would permit. A finer series of Roman Emperors I never saw anywhere, and the student in phrenology might, from their marked heads, read his lessons by the hour. There are also some rare fragments of important statues from the Stowe and Hertford galleries, several of which have been most shockingly repaired. Works like these should be placed in the best hands, or their mutilations remain unmeddled with. Topographically, certainly, but not with any reference to art, though some of the pictures are better than others, a very interesting gallery is in the course of formation, in which to assemble all the portraits of Westmoreland worthies, those of Hogarth of undying fame and Katharine Parr claiming our attention at once. Westmoreland may well feel proud of such a pair. The one as a painter of real life never equalled and rarely approached ; the other the great daughter of a great mother. The first Protestant Queen of England, who stood by and defended her faith with fearful risk, directly descended from the proud lineage of our Anglo-Saxon Kings, and the reddest Norman blood. The Protectress of Coverdale, the staunch friend of Ann Askern, the guide and counsellor of the studies of Lady Jane Grey, young Edward VI. and Elizabeth. But among "the Worthies" also were the two Whartons (Duke and Marquess) ; Dean Addison and Joseph ; Justice Wilson ; Watson, Bishop of Llandaff ; Waugh, of Carlisle ; and Sir George Fleming, of the same See ; Barrage, Archbishop of York ; Drs Burn, John Langhorn, and Shaw ; "Jockey" Bell ; George Clifford (Duke of Cumberland) ; Bernard Gilpin ; Admiral Pearson ; General Bowser and others. We walked upon the terrace afterwards, which is almost as celebrated as those at Duncombe Park, and on nearing it observed some fine yews, finer even than those at Byrom or Lord Coventry's place near Malvern. At last we came to Pooley Bridge, and as I could stand it no longer, while the horses bated the resources of my portmanteau came in useful, though there was far too little really warm clothing provided. Ullswater—which is nine miles by one, and therefore next to Windermere in size—begins here, and like the foot of almost every lake I know—at least any lake of pretension to size—it is tame in comparison to the head ; very good, no doubt, to those who live in a dismally flat country, but really nothing worth a second thought. At the little inn in former days I had an early experience of the district, and tasted lake trout for the first time there. Aye, and capital they were. They may talk of Loch Awe and Loch Leven fish as they like, but I'll back the Ullswater trout against all comers for flavour and condition in this or any other country. We soon arrived and halted at Lyulph's Tower, a shooting box built by the late Duke of Norfolk in Gowbarrow Park. Its name, like that of the lake, is referrable to Ulf or L'Ulf, the first Baron of Greystoke, of which property of the Howards the Park is a portion. The walk to Ara Force is but a short way, and of course we did it, notwithstanding the drought had rendered it as poor as poor could be, and the cold only made matters worse. The beautiful herd of cream-coloured West Highlanders, the troops of nervous fallow deer, the sweetness of the little glen, the freshness of the May, covering the thorns as with snow, and the charming scenery—for here Ullswater in fact assumes ascendency—were enough to warm us up into something like a sensation. But no; 'twas no use trying, nothing but dinner could avail; and Banting had ordered that some days ago for eight sharp. So into the carriage we bundled, as there were four miles further to travel, and it was late. However, sunless and wretched as it was, thence to our destination proved, how difficult soever it may be to make a distinction, where the pictures are so taking and so many, about the best thing we had done. In several portions of the way the Trossachs came so vividly to my recollection that it was almost impossible, but for the good road in place of the worst in Europe, to realize the fact of being elsewhere than in charming Perthshire. At length we drew up at Brownrigg's Hotel, in Patterdale, as the clock struck eight, so we had run it far too fine. The night being very raw, it was out of all question, reason, or common-sense to do without a fire—and we refused a down stairs room, after selecting another on the same floor with our sleeping apartments which adjoined it. Now then, Banting, let's know what they are going to give us, and his face (and mine too) was "quite a sight for to see" when the civilest and perhaps the best of all waiters remarked in the blandest manner, " Well, sir, yes, sir— there's trout, sir—you ordered it. Yes, sir; and sir, a fine piece of beef, sir—*would* you like anything else, sir?" Poor fellow, he appealed silently and imploringly to me, though all I could get out, being his guest, was—postpone the hour to nine sharp; allow the cook and ourselves time; it strikes me we might enjoy the luxury of beef at home, perhaps—trout, of course, but it can't be in better hands. Oh! mind order *the* puddings— " Patterdale puddings?" " Yes, sir." So here was another name, but very good they were, and so was the dinner, for the house is as well kept as any in the district; as for wine, the sherry, the hock, and the '51 Margeaux were about as topping as any man could serve, I don't care whether Paris and Company, Plews, Griffiths, Fennell, Tod Heatley, Thompson and Garthorne, Frank Greenwell, or any other man. Jones was learned about wines—he'd been in the country d'ye see, and agreed with me that few stomachs could stand Port if once it had been seen made. By the way, we had some Bucellas, that rejected and despised of all good stuff; when it's old and pure to start with, there's nothing better, and so it should—so—it—should —for hock grapes transplanted to such a climate only require care in manipulation, which they too seldom get, and hence the deterioration. The wine was excellent, and "the boy" told us George Croft, in Lisbon, supplied it sparkling, so we ordered some.

I find there are several methods of making these little pud-dings—no doubt each house-wife will have her own receipt, as in Scotland for haggis or in the North of England for yule cake and mince meat. Besides the receipt for Windermere or Pat-terdale or Castle puddings, mentioned in an earlier paper, the following are also noted in my own M.S. book :—Take four and-a-half ounces of flour, an equal quantity of ground rice, ten ounces of sugar, and half-a-dozen eggs. Beat the sugar and eggs well together, then add the flour and rice, a spoonful at a time, until all is consumed, beating all along and for three-quarters of an hour. Pour into cups, and before baking add (finely grated) the peel of half a lemon and the quarter of the juice. The other slightly differs, but each is worth trying. This is it :—Three eggs in the shell, equal weights of powdered loaf sugar and flour, and half the quantity of fresh butter. First melt the butter to oil, and then beat it thoroughly with the eggs to a cream, gradually adding the sugar and flour with lemon juice and grated peel at discretion. Half-fill coffee cups, bake moderately rather more than half an hour, and serve hot with Madeira sauce. The night was excessively raw, but the fare and fire resuscitated every one of us, and the evening passed rapidly away, conversation with unflagging smoothness flitting

"From grave to gay—from lively to severe."

Both Banting and "the boy" equally with myself delight in geography, and the study of the peopling of the West by the successive immigrations from the East, whence five big waves of population have rolled in, each by turn sweeping the mighty flood preceding it, further and still further on. The great Celtic inundation is the first we can distinctly trace as propelled by the irresistible force of the succeeding deluges of the Roman, the Teutonic, and the Sclave hordes, until it arrived at length into the far western extremities of Europe. These Celts being divided into two great branches—or rather distinct bodies—followed one another. Both spoke languages of a common stock, but distinguished by dialectic divergence as great as exist between Greek and Latin, or German and English, or Tuscan and Piedmontese. There are living languages to this day belonging to each of these branches. The first Gadhelic, or Gael, being represented by the Erse of Ireland, the Gaelic of Scotland (that in the west being by far the purest) and the Manx of the Isle of the Man ; the second, or Cymric, by the Welsh and the Armoricans of Brittany, still in well nigh exclusive use by a million and a half of Frenchmen. The Cymri, so it is said, issued from the Alpine region—the Gaels from the valleys of the Rhine and the Moselle, from which latter district it seems the earliest historic movements of the Celts took place. Three Celtic tribes burst over the Alps. They pillaged Rome, and after returning to Illyria for a while, broke in upon Greece and plundered the priceless treasures at Delphi. Settling for a time in Thrace, but ever restless, marauding, and aggressive, then crossing the Bosphorus, they took possession of the central region of Asia Minor, to which they gave the name of Galatea, or the land of the Gael, where also they long retained their Celtic speech and the ethenical peculiarities of their Celtic blood. There is no base on which to build conjecture as to the precise period or place or occasion when, where, or whence the two great divisions of the Celts took place. The most numerous people of Germany were the Gadhelic branch, and it may be inferred, from the fact of finding no names of the Cymric, Slavonic, or Teutonic stock, which have undergone phonetic changes in accordance with the genius of the Gaelic language, that the

Gaels found Germany unoccupied. Next came the Cymri, and they came as conquerors, though numerically much inferior to the Gaels. Lastly, the Germans from the North, in fewer numbers still, but still as conquerors, and they Germanised many Gadhelic names which previously had been Cymrycised. In the ancient parochial documents relating to several parishes north of the Forth, the gradual increase of the Teutonic element forms an interesting illustration of this early transitional period of history. In the Taxates of the 12th century, only $2\frac{1}{2}$ per cent. are Teutonic names, while in the Charterlaries, from the 12th to the 14th, the proportion rises to 4 per cent., and in the tax-rolls of 1554 to nearly 25. Even so late as the reign of Henry the Second, Hereford was considered to be in Wales—at least so says the Revd. Isaac Taylor in his *Words and Places*, p. 255, though he is contradicted by an able reviewer in the July number (231, p. 16) of the *Quarterly*—and it was not until Henry the Eighth's time that Monmouthshire became English. In Devon, the Cymric speech lingered till Elizabeth, and in Cornwall (where the dialect is very eccentric to this day) it was the only medium of conversation in her father's time. In the reign of Queen Anne, distinguished, as Mr Kirwan tells us, by an extraordinary burst of intellectual vigour, and great progress in the culinary art, it was confined to five or six villages in the western portion of that beautiful county, and it has only become extinct within the memory of living man, while the Celtic race still survive the absorption of their mother tongue with little admixture of the Teutonic strain.

In Wales one observes the change of language accompanied by a very partial infusion of Saxon blood, and even in Mercia and Wessex the bulk of the people is of the pure Celtic strain. In Glamorgan, Flint, Denbigh, and part of Montgomery, English has almost entirely supplanted the native language, those clinging to it, except in the rarest instances, understanding if not speaking ours : in the other border counties, also, it is rapidly dying out, very much as one observes it even in the most tenacious and remote parts of Ireland and Scotland, as applied to Erse and Gaelic.

The Saxon keels cannot have transported any numerous population, and the ceorls or churls were no doubt the pure-blooded descendants of the Celts of Britain. The Celtic element in the population was large, and long remained unabsorbed by the Saxon ; and it is worthy of remark that over the whole land almost all the river and shire names contain Celtic roots, as do likewise a fair sprinkling of those of hills, valleys, and fortresses. Comparative analyses are the readiest reckoners, and Banting seems to have a perfect system of them at command. He furnished me with this, which shews at a glance the proportion of Saxon, Danish, and Celtic names of hills, hamlets, woods, villages, &c., in the various places detailed :—

Percentage of names from the	Suffolk.	Surrey.	Devon.	Cornwall.	Monmouth.	Isle of Man.	Ireland.
Celtic	2	8	32	80	76	59	80
Anglo-Saxon	90	91	65	20	24	20	10
Norse	8	1	3	0	0	21	1

By far the larger number of Celtic names in England are distinctly of the Cymric type. These Cymri, by some considered to be the Picts, held the Lowlands of Scotland up to the Perthshire Hills, until the Scots crossed over from Ireland (then called Scotia, and North Britain Nova Scotia) to Argyle, and extended their dominions over the whole of the North-west of the kingdom, encroaching largely on the Cymri. In the 12th century the Clyde and Forth were the southern boundaries of what was called Scotland ; and now when treaties are being torn by the mere fact of aggressive war, and the landmarks of Europe wrenched out of their old places, it is somewhat interesting to review the former condition of our own neighbourhood, so comparing the past with the present.

May 22nd.—Up by times. The fragrant freshness of the day realised to the full Milton's apothegm —

> Sweet is the breath of morn ; her rising sweet,
> With charm of earliest birds ;

and the loveliness of the situation in which Banting had pitched our comfortable tent could not possibly have been seen to more advantage. Browrigg's Hotel is five minutes' walk to the head of the lake. Bouass' house is not only a much larger building, but at the very water's edge a mile off. There seems a good deal of rivalry between the establishments, both of which are considered good ; though from experience I can only form an opinion of the management and purveyance of that in which we were, and which is excellent in all respects. It struck me as, without any comparison, much the more beautifully placed of the two. The perfection of the day went far no doubt in exciting our elastic feelings. "The boy" and I strolled out long before our host had even commenced his elaborate toilet, much less finished that apparently tedious operation, and as he had ordered breakfast the night before, the brace of us had a pleasant constitutional ramble. The contrast between this day and yesterday materially assisted the brightness of everything around us, and the reflection is not a little humiliating that one so soon forgets blessings just experienced. The weather had been exceptionally delicious for any season both before and since Tuesday, for May in the Lake district nothing had been known like it ; yet the moment it varied on Saturday nothing could be more miserable than our feelings, which were now as happily reversed when it turned again. The garden attached to the Hotel presented natural capabilities a fortune could not transplant or establish, and the peeps we obtained on all sides were perfect. At one o'clock we turned out for a walk until 7 30, and by the direction of the invaluable waiter, who kindly supplied a capital field glass, we took the path to Blowick, past the slate quarry. It was exactly one of those rare days in which it was preferable to moon about and loll, even on high ground, inhaling the soft breath of moor air, while basking in the glowing warmth, rather than travel. A rare day, was it not ? and then the views from a' top of Blowick ! Seated among the rocks and junipers, the Lake far away below, its waters and the cloudless sky of deep pure blue, no *dolce far niente* could be more composing. The pretty little church, in the churchyard of which is railed round a curiously knarled and hollow ancient yew centuries

of age, Patterdale Hall, embedded in ornamental timber, a glen
opening up, and studded with a mining village, the other hotel
and our own, Gowborrow Park, a long reach of all the best part
of Ullswater, Kirkstone Pass, where an eagle was seen so late
as 1850, a perfect amphitheatre of rugged mountains, and un-
dulating ground richly wooded and fat with pastures, such was
the scene about us, unequalled to my mind without any comparison in the district. The parsley fern, flourishing perfectly
unshaded, abounded ; that curious little plant the butterburr was
also plentiful, and many others we gathered and brought home.
In one of the fir plantations we observed the young cones—six
inches long at least—clustered in masses together, and of a
colour so superb they could be distinguished at a considerable
distance in the bright sunlight. Oddly enough it was one of
the brilliant tints introduced this year as the Garibaldi ombre,
and is the combination of amythest and ruby. Banting was
very learned about the monks of old who belonged to Furness
Abbey, worked minerals here, and no doubt enjoyed the trout ;
and, if they had time for anything in the way of comfort, the
Northmen must have revelled in the fastnesses and retreats of
this one of their most favourite nooks. For three whole centuries, from the 8th to the 11th, these hardy vagabonds pursued
their restless harry, and became an established terror to western
Europe, sacking, burning, ravishing, and murdering, whither-
soever they went. They piloted their barks up the shoally
and the shallow Elbe, the Scheldt, the Rhine, the Neckar, and
the Moselle. They ravaged the sweet valleys of the Somme,
the Soane, the Marne, the Loire, and the Garonne. They
besieged Paris, Amiens, Tours, Troyes, Chalons, Poictiers,
Bordeaux, Toulouse, and London repeatedly. One of the big
lions guarding the Arsenal at Venice, and once adorning Athens,
is deeply grooved and scored with Norse Runes, recording the
capture of the Piræus by Harald Hardráda, or Haardraade,
the doughty Norwegian king, who, with Toste, in 1066 fell at
Stamford Bridge, after flaunting his celebrated banner—Landöde
(the land ravager)—in his expeditions to the East against the
Saracens, and real or fictitious enemies of Christianity, his zeal
impelled him to worry and hunt down. They established
themselves as conquerors or colonists over fully the half of
England, in the Hebrides, and Western coasts of Scotland, in
Greenland, Iceland, the Isle of Man, and the north of France.
They did more, they founded kingdoms in this country, and in
Ireland, in France, Naples, and in Sicily, while a Norse dynasty
ruled Russia for 700 years, and for centuries the Varangian
guard upheld the throne of the Byzantine Emperors. There
were principal Danish stations at Deptford, Woolwich, and
Greenwich. The fens which bordered the Witham, the Welland,
and the Nen, was the southern boundary of these settlers. The
Danelag, or district, was divided by agreement between Alfred
and Gudrum from the Saxon by a line passing along the
sea and the Ouse, and then following to the north-east of
Watlinga or Watling-street. North of the Tweed they entirely
disappear, except in the north-west, and there are very few
Norse names in Durham and Northumberland ; indeed only 23
and 22 respectively, as against 142 in Cumberland, 153 in
Westmoreland, 292 in Lincolnshire, and 405 in Yorkshire, out

F

of the 1,500 in all England. There were Danish fortresses at Leicester, Derby, Stamford, Nottingham, Lincoln and York, and in the same way that the Danish names in England are seen to radiate from the Wash, so the Norwegian immigration seems to have proceeded from Morecombe Bay and that portion of the coast facing the Isle of Man. Cumberland and Westmoreland contain far more Norwegian than Danish names, and the Lake District was well nigh exclusively peopled by the former people, so that while their suffixes—gill—garth—thwaite —force—fell—dale—tarn—beck—are abundant, as well as "by," meaning a town or village, and purely Danish, and hence a paradox, the Danish forms of thorpe—toft—haugh —with—næs—ey—are almost unknown, and the Anglo-Saxon test-words—ham—ford—worth—and ton are comparatively rare. More than 150 distinct personal names of the Icelandic type are preserved in the local topography of the Lake district, and the commonest names in Iceland are Kettle, Halle, Ormur, Gils ; whence spring Kettlewell, Hallthwaite, Ormethwaite, Gilstone, and Gilsland. By far the most prevalent Christian names there are Olafur, borne by 992 persons, Einer by 878, and Bjarni by 869 ; which are reproduced in Ulverstone, Eunerdale, and Barneyhouse. Hrani or Rennie is found in Ransdale, Rennerdale, Ransbarrow, and Wrenside ; Loki in Lockthwaite and Lockholm ; Buthar in Buttermere, Butterhill, and Buttergill ; and Skögul in Skeggleswater. So much for the local Icelandic derivations. In other parts, Grimsby, Burnthwaite, Harrowby, Thoresby, Haccoxby, and Guttersby are traced up to Grim, Biörn, Harold, Thor, Haco, and Gudor. The Norsemen called the Hebrides the Sudreyjar, or the Southern Islands, and the two Sees of the Sudreyjar (founded in 838) and Man were united in the 11th century, and made dependent on the Archbishop of Trondhjem, in Nerway, by whose hand, and that of his successors till 1334, the prelates of that See, which "is better than nothing," as Sidney Smith said, were consecrated. In 1380, the Bishopric of Man was separated, but all subsequent appointments have been made under the joint title of Sodor and Man, so long under the care of a Presbyterian Church. All interested in these northern people—and despite their insensate obstinacy, who is not in the Danes now, or who that has visited their country in the Norwegians, too—should read Worsaae's "Account" of them, as well as Ferguson's, and Lord Ellesmere's Guide to Northern Archæology, at whose and his brother's (the late Duke of Sutherland) suggestion the first author visited this country. The Vikings, pronounced Veeklngs, so called from the Icelandic Vik, a creek or bay of the sea, or the Danish Vig, battle or slaughter, were terrible fellows, and played the most conspicuous part in the Danish conquest ; but sea rovers and pirates though they were, I now never think of them without delight after that little Prussian business, which, by the way, suggested the verse in Mr Speciall's cheery Shakespearian song at our Local Celebration dinner on the 12th of May last, which runs thus—

" The health of the Prince and his lovely bride,
    Who to English fortunes her lot has tied ;
    Toast her old home—' the Danish land ;'
    Drink to the fleet, with Vikings mann'd,
    That sent the base Germans to Heligoland."

Vive le, Vive le, Vive le Vin,
Vive le, Vive le, Vive le Chant,
Vive le, Vive le, Vive le Vin,
    et Vive la Compagnie."˙

In an ancient Scandinavian Biblical paraphrase Goliath is
called a Viking. I much mistake the signs of the times if
Germany will not 'ere long discover that wickedness like hers
never yet triumphed over public opinion. She has had her
little foray and her cruel wrong, but another degradation is at
hand. God grant it soon, for Jutland can only look to Heaven
for retribution, though "curses like chickens return to roost,"
while there is an "inexorable logic of facts," an inevitable
corollary therefrom, and the undying justice of cause and effect.
Both Austria and Prussia still groan under their chastisement
by the first Napoleon, whose violence they have eclipsed without his brilliancy. May they from his example soon realise
that acts of injustice, such as theirs upon the weak and brave,
may cause a severe retaliation from the strong, and that the
wrongs of the pettiest state may lead to a conflagration in
Europe, in which they will be the first to suffer the overdue
penalty of illegitimate aggression.

Nothing seemed so strange to me as the almost total absence
of visitors. To be sure, they said "the season" had not commenced, as if that was any excuse for not taking advantage of
such weather. Well, we are very much creatures of habit, and
even yet we find some methodical folks who adopt the detestable system of "dressing the grate," mindful only of a fixed
date, and regardless of all comfort if the weather be change-
able or unseasonable, as it often is. At Brownrigg's there were
only two parties--our own and another, but it was large--Man-
chester people come to spend the Sunday, and very happy they
all looked, especially a young couple, evidently on the eve of
marriage. In the afternoon, they filled a special coach inside
and out, so we were left alone. No season can come wrong
among the lakes. Both Yorick and Banting were at Keswick
last winter. They skated on Derwentwater, and the ice was
like glass—a great mirror laid flat amidst the frosted scenery—
yet nobody goes then. It is the same, in May; if possible,
more brilliant still, owing to the color and the hope of Spring.
Nor yet in Autumn! Is it not strange? I don't know any
tour which can be done more cheaply and better for the money
than that of the English lakes. This little jaunt of ours was
not an example of my meaning, mind, because, being out of
the season, and no coaches on the road, we had invariably to
post whenever hiring was necessary, whilst our living was
luxurious ; but if you content yourselves with coffee-room fare,
which is unusually good, and avoid private apartments, which
are of course expensive, the thing may be done comfortably and
well for 7s 3d a-day ! 'Tis surprising how they do it, but
they do. Now, I asked for this information at the George,
and Miss Beethom told me that 2s for breakfast, 1s 9d for
meat tea, 2s for bed, and 1s 6d for service, was their regular
tariff, and the usual price thereabouts. Beer and wine
naturally are extra, but the two meals mentioned are so sub-

˙ Appendix.

stential, so nicely served, and with such variety, that no man, not even a schoolboy, need have more. Why on the 26th and 7th of this month Mr and Mrs Bowman, of Gainford, had a wonderful trip with 86 of their pupils at a cost of a crown a head ! Such an effort could only be accomplished by energy and youth. To Clifton by rail—thence they walked to Pooley Bridge—thence by boats to Lyulph's Tower, Gowborrow Park, and Ara Force, and so on to Patterdale, where they had one of these meat teas, after which the very walk we took was accomplished. How Brownrigg put them all up is only accounted for by a mutual and pleasantly natural desire for accommodation ; it is astonishing what any of us can and will do if we like. However, there they all slept, and rose with the lark as fresh as paint, for young stomachs know no fatigue, so that by six o'clock, after breakfast, the lot started for Helvellyn. The young 'uns tailed off at quarter distance, and no wonder, for even pluck gives in to lack of thew ; but the big lads, with their master and the guide, in all thirty, passing over Squirrel Edge, completed their task, and were enchanted with the view of Windermere, Grassmere, and Ullswater from the summit of Catchedecam, the utmost peak of the mountain it is safe to attempt. Returning by coaches and 'bus to Pooley, where a cold collation awaited their arrival, the whole party then retook the train at Clifton and reached home at six that evening. There's expedition and economy for you. The coach-fares are very reasonable, too, and when the railway is opened that item of cost will be reduced, but the whole tour is so much within a ring fence that a fortnight will suffice for leisure in the whole of it, notwithstanding a month or two might be most enjoyably occupied daily. No doubt, roaming far away from home excites its own peculiar zest, which no one more than myself appreciates ; but the longer I live, and the more I see, the fact is forced uppermost that we really, as a nation, see too little of what is well worth attention in our own country. "Those nearest to church are last in," is true all the whole world over, and the idea of the ability to visit home scenes at any time often excuses postponement ; but in our distant wanderings we certainly are too prone to ignore, or rather perhaps to underrate the charms of the lake and coast scenery, and the sylvan loveliness of Great Britain and Ireland, as well as the endless variety our rivers afford. We are too apt to strain after the attainment of distance rather than the scrutiny of objects, which, to be seen well, should be examined, pondered over, and reflected upon.

The people of the hotel seemed to understand us much better to-day than when they thought the " beautiful piece of beef" would suit our host's fastidious palate, and really nothing could be nicer than the delicate fare served. Early in the morning " the boy" and I inspected the fresh-caught trout. Mr Brownrigg has an extensive take of fishing, and is able to supply his customers on the shortest notice. None of the weights are great in any of these lakes, nothing approaching those in the Scotch or the Italian, where I have known trout 30, and even up to 45lb. ; but for flavour, those of Ullswater surpass any I ever tasted. They are very handsome and well grown, and the spots are larger, more distinct, and separate than any other breed.

What a night it was ! just such as would follow such a day, and not a veil of fog or vapour.

"But look ! the moon in silver mantle clad,
Walks o'er the dew of yon high eastern hill."

At full, she hung suspended in mid-air, no breath of wind disturbing the calm of all around. We could not shut out scenery we enjoyed so much from both the windows, which framed each view as a picture, so to speak, but discussed the monks again, and the Margeaux too. Banting is the quaintest dog for scraps of information, as well as real, solid, stiff research. We laughed again and again—I believe "the boy" almost cried at some of the items—when, with the utmost solemnity, our host illustrated the subject with Jacques Tasquin's little bill for some decorations he had carried out for a monastery in Flanders, as he said, " at a remote period of history—but it is a perfectly authentic document." The amount was 78 florins 10 sous, and the particulars ran thus : —

		fl.	s.
1.—Correcting and varnishing the Ten Commandments	..	5	12
2.—Embellished Pontius Pilate, and put a new ribbon on his hat	..	3	6
3.—Put a new tail to St. Peter's cock, and mended his crest	..	2	3
4.—Refixed the good thief to the cross, and gave him a new finger	..	1	7
5.—Refeathered and gilt the left wing of the angel Gabriel		14	18
6.—Washed the servant maid of the High Priest Caiphas and put colour on her cheeks	..	5	14
7.—Renewed the sky, added two stars, gilt the sun, and cleaned the moon	..	7	14
8.—Revived the flames of Purgatory, and restored some souls	..	6	6
9.—Revived the fire of hell, put a new tail on Lucifer, mended his left claw, and did several things for the damned	..	4	10
10.—Put a new border to Herod's robe, gave him two teeth and readjusted his wig	..	2	2
11.—Put a piece on Haman's leather breeches, and put two buttons on his waistcoat	..	2	3
12.—Put new gaiters on Tobias's son, travelling with the Angel Gabriel ; and a new belt to his travelling bag		2	5
13.—Cleaned the ears of Balaam's ass, and shod him	..	3	7
14.—Put ear-rings on Sarah	..	2	0
15.—Put a new stone in David's sling, enlarged the head of Goliath, and bent back his legs	..	3	1
16.—Put new teeth in the jaw-bone of the ass of Sampson		1	5
17.—Pitched Noah's ark, and gave him a new pair of sleeves		6	0
18.—Put a piece on the shirt of the prodigal son, washed the pigs, and put water in their troughs	..	3	4
19.—Put a handle to the Samaritan's cruse	..	1	5
Total		78	10

We got on talking, comparing the merits of various musicians, and seemed finally agreed that Felix Mendelssohn presented the rarest combination of talent yet produced, and stood alone in his art, as Shakespeare in his own. In him you have the massiveness of Handel, the tenderness of Mozart, the sweetness of Purcell and of Arne, the brilliancy of Rossini, the rythmetical melody of Meyerbeer, Haydn, and Auber; in fact, the influence of all schools with poetry, descriptive power, and variety infinite. His Elijah* led us on to the Priest of Baal—

* Appendix.

their worship and their wilfulness. Thus pleasantly did our last evening float away. Bauting read aloud Wordsworth's "Peter Bell," which he and most consider the happiest effort of this fascinating poet, though I'm all for his ode on "Westminster Bridge," but when he came to—

> "And he had trudged through Yorkshire dales,
>   Among the rocks and winding scars,
> Where deep and low the hamlets lie
> Beneath their little patch of sky
> And little lot of stars"—

I had almost to give in.

What I noticed in this hotel was that brown bread was not to be had, and even the white was inferior. Now that's odd, is it not? There cannot surely be any difficulty about the matter, but she is not the first good cook I have known who overlooks the importance of bread making, which only requires such ordinary ability that failure is like bad spelling and a positive disgrace while good is no credit. She gave us some excllent macaroni *au gratin*, which, however, is not half so good as Mrs Howcroft's receipt for doing it white—nay, nor a twentieth part as good. The clover body gave it to me the other day at Darlington, where she lives, and I am glad to find "goes out." Being placed unreservedly at my disposal publication of the secret is no breach of good faith, so here it is:—Stew well until thoroughly tender 4 ounces of macaroni in weak stock, add one ounce of grated cheese, a tea spoonful of dry mustard, an idea of pepper and salt, a dessert spoonful of flour, and a little good cream ; then serve in a hot water dish if you have one. Perhaps she has some wondrous subtle mode in the manipulation, or perhaps it is just as easy to do well as making melted butter, in which more cooks fail than otherwise ; but no one ever made better macaroni in my experience, and very few so good, so that I well may thank her for her kindness in telling me so simple a method of dressing one of the most nutritious and palatable dishes that comes to table at any time of day or night.

May 23rd.

> Then let the world jog along as it will,
> We'll be free and easy still ;
>   Free and easy,
>   Free and easy,
> We'll be free and easy still.

So runs the melodious chorus of a jolly old song, equalling in sweetness, though it is impossible to surpass, those one hears in Huddersfield and that ilk from Yorkshire throats. We sang it—aye, we sang it cheerily—on the 29th ult. (July) at the parting dinner to an honoured guest*—one of that rare sort tritely and justly designated by an accomplished speaker, who can think on his legs—an advantage, like good reading, by far too little cultivated—as "a sage amongst men—a lad with bairns —very Cupid with the ladies ;" and this reminds me that our pleasant trip approached its end. "The boy" and I awaited the arrival of the take of trout, and selected enough for Yorick and for home. The hotel master charged 1s a pound, which

* Appendix.

struck me as a groat too much, and no less than 10s 6d per
tambourine. Why that's the price for char! Well, he said,
they are just as good; see how pink they are. Oh! yes, the
colour's all right, no doubt; and they are oftener sold for char
than char, if men are not wide awake; but the price is absurd.
So we left them. By seven, Jones had breakfasted and was off. We
postponed our meal till eleven, and found the change to Rigg's,
at Windermere, very much for the worse—but I must not anti-
cipate. By the way, both my friends say that "the boy," instead of being "above the middle height, yet not tall," is good
six feet, though he don't look it; so thick and mouldy, well-
proportioned all over, like a clever cob he is, and very bad to
match. About the same time he left we ensconced ourselves in
a light wagonette behind as fast a pair of posters as one
need wish to see. Tight 'uns they were for the job, as our route
lay right up Kirkstone pass, at the summit of which there is a
stone

——— "whose church-like frame
Gives to the savage pass its name."

The road they say is the highest in England, and upon its
crest is the highest inhabited house. It's very cold up here in
winter, Sir, the poor woman said, aye and starving enough
this very morning. Right glad we were of the buffalo robe
of silver wolf, which had been sent after us with kind forethought
from the George; it was fit for the Emperor of all the Russias, or
even that Magician, who can conjure millions out of discredit,
the financial Chase. It drizzled too, so out came Banting's
wonderful umbrella, and my poor old Sarie Gamp, which
horrified him; but she's quite good enough for me, and better
than his jemmy affair, as no one falls in love with her. Looking
back ever and anon, and looking forward now, the scene from
that vast height was great. The mountains and the little hills
lay tossed about in wild confusion, and one could see the sea,
they said, into Scotland, too, and over islet-dotted Windermere. We had sunshine enough yesterday for many a day,
and the sullenness of all around after it had got out fair was
grand. What a spot for the rites of Baal this must have been,
and was. Why the remnants of the ordeal by fire have scarcely
died out yet in that most superstitious of Counties, in which a
man dare at his peril cry "Cuckoo" in Borrowdale. During this
drive I was struck with the children clustering about the
carriage, or running in the hope of coppers, just as they used
to do in Ireland before the famine, which I witnessed. What
a sight of woe and want was that, indeed! The men and
women wan and wasted, stricken down and thudded, crawling
shadows of their former selves—the children with their pro-
truding, sightless eyes, swollen bellies, withered haunches, and
limbs no thicker than their bones. The whole country looked
cursed, Godforgotten, lost and dreary even in the mocking
sunshine in its loveliest parts I had known in happier days.
Death, stalking as he did, mowing down his thousands in a
week, was in truth a blessing, when life was utter desolation.

At length the sun dissipated the vapour, and in descending
Troutbeck, the ever-changing lovely valley enchanted us by its
exquisite variety. Such ferns there were, and miles of under-
wood of brilliant broom, like Californian gold amongst the

freshest green about. Hence it was that Hogarth sprang, or rather here and at Kirby Thore his people lived, though he himself was born in London. As an engraver, a painter, a humorist of the highest order, and the most genial friend, his fame will be familiar as household words, so long as a relish for English art exists. The named is derived from högardr—an enclosure for hay—and the old family were well-to-do 'statesmen. The graceful lines Garrick wrote, and had engraved upon the tomb at Chiswick, bespeak at once the author and the artist :—

> Farewell, great painter of mankind,
> Who reach'd the noblest point of wit :
> Whose pictured morals charm the mind,
> And through the eye correct the heart.
> If genius fire thee, reader, stay ;
> If nature touch thee, drop a tear ;
> If neither move thee, turn away,
> For Hogarth's honoured dust lies here.

The sun made it delightfully hot as we rattled along this happy valley; and at last we came to the border of the lake, which Banting dilated upon as having originally been spelt Winandermere, and combated the received derivation of Gwyndur-mere — meaning clear water — as the Celts invariably put their qualifying word last. Which was correct made little difference in its beauty—though mind it is inferior to Patterdale—but our conversation soon followed a groove into which mine host slid as it were by nature and inclination. Buttermere might be, he said, Booth-tor-mere, the lake of the village on the hill as Wordsworth has it ; yet his opinion inclined to that of Ferguson, who considers that the old Norse hero, Buthar Lipr, from whom Butter lip llaw takes its name, has something to do with it. Brothers-water we passed on the road, is from Broad dur or Broad water—and it is a tarn just about square. The distinctive difference between a tarn, the Scandinavian spelling of which is tjörn or tjarn, and a lake is that it has no visible inlet or supply, being simply the result of day water, natural drainage, and the weeping from rocks — hence its name, the Danish word taar being almost our own tear. Many of these lake-names have personal associations, and many are purely descriptive. Crummock Water, for instance, originally Crumbeck, is compounded of beck and Krumr, a proper name. In old Norse the final r after a consonant was not pronounced, and merely signified the nominative case. Again, Ambleside, originally Hamelside (where, by-the-bye, Scott has erected one of his best churches), in like manner is the habitation of Hamel. Grassmoor, Grasmere, and Grisedale are referable to swine ; Gris being the old Saxon for wild pig, which haunted these places. Old man from Alt man, or high mountain. Bassenthwaite from Bassing and thwaite, the habitation of this family, or rather the descendants of Bass, the Saxon patronymic ing being the same as Mac or O', meaning sons or issue. Derwent water from the Celtic Dur (clear), and guyn (water). Some will have it that the river Derwent is the winding water, but there are many of that name, few of which are particularly tortuous, though all are clear. Penrith signifies the hill of the ford, though it is usually given as red hill, which Banting declares to be incorrect. Keswick, formerly Keldswicke, means the place of the springs by the water; and, remembering Horne Tooke's remark, "Letters, like soldiers, are apt to drop off on a long march," the original orthography has been well preserved. Patterdale, with its well dedicated to St. Patrick, has reference to him. Then as to the names of mountains. The King of Saxony, a learned authority on these subjects, derives Blencathra from blein (shiny), and cathara (rugged), and it answers that description, the mica in its formation being brilliant in its early stages of degradation. Mell fell is from the proper name Mjöll (meaning fresh snow), and is sometimes spelt Maol fell; the Norwegian Mel Fjeld and the Icelandic Mæli Fell corresponding, the meol, a windmill, having nothing to do with it, though the usually accepted base. Scratch Meal Scar is undoubtedly from Skratti, a demon, hence our "old Scratch;" and mella is ancient Norse for an evil spirit closely related to Mjöll, in fact his twin brother. The theory of deriving names of places from two or more distinct languages is now common, but dangerous on the face of it. An exception in Dunmail Raise, however, presents itself, the former, being unmistakeably British, should have had cairn after instead of Raise, which is pure Scandinavian, meaning the same thing so far as the pile of stones goes, though the *raise* was always to indicate a grave beneath, and the cairn oftener a landmark or memorial—witness that to the Prince Consort at Balmoral as the latest instance. And so on, *ad infinitum*. For Christian names the Yankees exceed all nations in eccentricities and ugliness. I have known families distinguished by letters of the alphabet, the K Smiths, for instance, being thus picked out of the herd from the A's, B's, &c. There is a family in Michigan whose sons were named One Stickney, Two Stickney, Three Stickney, and whose daughters were called First Stickney, Second Stickney, and so on Three elder children of a family in Vermont were christened Joseph, And, Another; and it is supposed that, should they have any more, they might have named them Also, Moreover, Nevertheless, and Notwithstanding. Another family actually named their child Finis, supposing that it was their last; but they afterwards happened to have a daughter and two sons, whom they called Addenda, Appendix, and Supplement. Another parent set out to perpetuate the twelve apostles, and named the fifth child Acts. A man in Pennsylvania called his second son James Also, and the third William Likewise. Following out this favourite study of Banting, I have long taken an interest in names, and once made a list from observation of odd instances, those in Devon being by far the quaintest. It is curious to observe there are above a quarter of a million of persons in England and Wales bearing the cosmopolitan surname of Smith, and above 45,000 persons in Scotland. If you meet 73 persons in England, or even 68 in Scotland, you may expect to find a Smith among them. Next to Smith there comes in each country a purely local name— Jones in England and Wales, Macdonald in Scotland; in every 78 persons in Scotland there is a Macdonald. The next most common names in England are :—Williams, Taylor, Davies, and Brown; in Scotland, Brown occupies a very high numerical position, but several purely Scottish names also stand high upon the list—Robertson, Stewart, Campbell, Anderson. There is a much greater clan predominance of surnames in Scotland than in England. There are in both countries many surnames derived from occupation, locality, or personal qualities ; while in England in the 50 most common surnames only 27, in Scotland 37—the great majority—are real patronymics and truly sirenames, either in their pure unaltered state, as Grant, Cameron, &c., or altered so as to express the descent, as in Robertson and Morrison, or with the Gaelic Mac. A recent examination of the birth-register of Scotland for a year showed 104,018 births and only 6,823 separate surnames ; so that there are more than 15 persons, upon an average, to a surname, or only 6·5 surnames to 100 persons. In England, a similar examination by the Registrar-General showed only 8·4 persons to a surname, or 12 surnames to 100 persons. The proportion of persons attached to each surname would have been still larger in Scotland, and more than double that of England, but for the immense immigration from Ireland in the last quarter of a century. In the Scottish registers the 50 most common surnames embrace nearly 30 per cent. of all the names on the register ; in England only about 18 per cent. Of the 50 most common surnames in Scotland, 32 either entirely or in the form in which they occur in Scotland may be reckoned as having originated in that country, and as being peculiar to it—a very large proportion considering all circumstances. The remainder are common also to England. The *sobriquets* perpetuated as surnames from a supposed likeness to the animal creation of course vary in England and Scotland with the language of each country. English Fox is superseded in Scotland by Tod, a very common name, having the same meaning. Bullock becomes Stott, and Crow Craw. Hogg in Scotland is not to be traced to pig, but a lamb a year old. Mr Stork, of the Scottish register-office, from whose sixth annual report (just issued) these statements are taken, has also had the curiosity to note the Christian names occurring upon the registers. In 3,690 entries of births of boys there were only 67 different Christian names, but among a like number of girls there were 86. John and James greatly preponderate among the boys. Among the girls Margaret is the favourite name, but Mary is very close to it. In the Highland clans Mary decidedly preponderates, but Margaret in all other parts of Scotland. Several names not uncommon among girls in England did not occur so many as three times in the entire Scottish list of 3,689—Beatrice, Clara, Emma, Julia, Lucy ; and among the 3,690 boys there were not three with either of several of our common English names— Alfred, Arthur, Benjamin, Frederick, Philip, Stephen. The girls' list shows many variations from what we should find in England ; there are twice as many Elspeths as Emilys, twice as many Marjorys as Louisas, four times as many Euphemias as Harriets, five times as many Graces as Carolines.

Well, at length we reached the well-kept villas clustering about Windermere, and were soon set down at Rigg's Hotel, from which the view is so fine. ·What the private apartments may command, I know not, though some friends we found there said their breakfast was capital ; our's in the coffee-room was execrable in every way. We strolled down to the lake, past

Spencer Hall's hydropathic establishment, and found its surface crowded with empty boats, "as the season had not commenced," notwithstanding such weather. From its natural formation the lake district is, of course, generally moist, and some idea may be formed from the fact that at Seathwaite, in Borrowdale, no less than 35 inches of rain fell last September (1863). What fell at Keswick during May of that year, I have been unable accurately to make out, but this year the table is as follows, and without any parallel, they tell me. Nay, such a season they have had during the whole of June and the better half of July, when we were shivering on the east side of the island, as is not in the memory of living man. We all remember the strawberries without flavor, and the hay without fragrance; in fact, vegetation halted rather than progressed till St. Swithin came, and ever since then the drought has been as destructive as the withering cold. Turnips don't grow, peas don't fill, nor potatoes swell; the brittle stalks of the light-eared corn, blighted with black lice and red robin, snap prostrate and wasted by the electric gusts. Lean stock is a drug, and fat at prices fabulous. The wells fail, and springs, hitherto inexhaustible, cease their welcome health-bestowing flow. Farmers—with true English privilege, ever grumbling, though ever genial—may well look glum; and so may we, for the year will be short—very short indeed. Even the foliage, frizzled on the trees, falls 'ere its due time, or rattles in the air. July, as we all know, is usually wet, and to shew the gage this year, Mr Plant, M.B.M.S., says that at Birmingham the fall of rain there that month—0·7 inch—was less than in any previous July since 1825, when only 0·32 inch was collected! For another comparison we must go back to 1800. The summer of 1826 was very dry; only 0·53 inch of rain fell there in two months ending July 1, but the country suffered more from intense heat than drought. There was more rain in July, 1826, than in the same month in 1825. At Brackley, Northamptonshire, August 6, at 3 p.m., the temperature of the air was 75 deg., while the dew point (that is, the temperature to which a body must be reduced in order for the moisture in the atmosphere to begin to condense upon it) was as low as 47½ deg., or 27½ deg. lower than the air temperature. The atmosphere near the surface of the earth contained at the time only 33 per cent. of the vapour of water that it was capable of holding. The wind was north-westerly and moderate, the barometer stood at 20·65 inches, and the sky brilliantly clear.* But here's the table taken at Keswick:—

							Inches.
		Rainfall, May 1864.					
May 2nd	..	..	..	..	..	..	·582
" 3rd	..	..	..	..	..	..	·174
" 4th	..	..	..	..	..	..	·150
" 6th	..	..	..	..	..	..	·148
" 7th	..	..	..	..	..	..	·470
" 21st	..	..	..	..	..	..	·130
" 29th	..	..	..	..	..	..	·145
" 31st	..	..	..	..	..	..	·250
Total	..	..	..	..	..	..	2·049

The month of May, 1863, was unusually fine, yet that of this

* Appendix.

year surpassed it, as the following extract from Mr Fletcher's " Meteorological Journal " at Tarnbank, proves :—

Date.	Temperature.						Rain.
	Max.	Min.	Mean Max.	Mean Min.	Range.	Mean Temp.	Inches
May, 1863..	62·8 ..	36·0 ..	54·5 ..	42·9 ..	26·8 ..	48·72 ..	3·756
May, 1864..	78·0 ..	36·3 ..	59·9 ..	43·6 ..	41·7 ..	51·60 ..	2·264

The thermometers are standards by Negretti and Zambra, and are four feet above the ground.

'Ere we went down to the station, Banting received a telegraphic summons to the West Riding, so instead of driving to Keswick we had each other's company so far as Darlington, where we terminated our trip by a little dinner at the King's Head. I ordered it by telegraph from Tebay. " Dinner for three at seven sharp to-night. I bring fish." Is that all, he said, and where's the third ? All I quite enough for so good a caterer as you'll see the landlady is. The new tenants are gathering money like hay, and will make their fortunes if they stand corn. As for the odd man, George here will join us, and we will to give you the best dinner we can get. He's fresh from the Sportsman at Caernarvon, though his healthy appetite did not require the good training of that excellent house to enjoy the fare to-night. There was only an hour before the mail train time, but we did a vast deal of execution in sixty minutes. Really, folks may think we were bagmen, " boxing Harry," and out for the week ; but it is pleasant now and then to sing with " our own Sweet Will,"

Then heigh ho ! the holly !
The holly !
This life is most jolly,
Most jolly.

They are welcome to every speculation within their power, as it does not affect the point one whit. We had a few days of real enjoyment, for which my thanks are due to a couple of as hospitable and as intelligent fellows as are out, and whose kindness I can never forget. If anybody else has my luck, may the same feelings be excited—so now. But what on earth should we have done without these public-houses, so reviled by a well-meaning and industrious party, capable of so much good by their admirable organization, yet effecting so little ? We should have been wholly incompetent to derive amusement for want of home comforts, and hence the rapid interchange of passing thoughts would have been impossible. True, everything depends upon the choice of our companions in a tour. We must have originality — similarity of taste—and that freshness—that vigour of mind and determination to make the best of whatever comes uppermost. Of course you must ; but suppose for a moment, instead of being treated as we were at the George and at Brownrigg's, the tariff had been reversed—the women crabbed, the waiters crusty, and the *menus* miserable ! Does any one in his senses believe we could have been so blithe and hearty as we were? Not a bit of it — we should never have been in form at all. As it was, we made the most of it ; and let each who can follow the example—that's all I have got to say. These two hotels are not so large as those at Grasmere, Low Wood, Portinscale,

Windermere, Ullswater, or Bowness ; but I'll back their service
to be incomparably better, judging from my friends' experience
and my own at various times. The only parallel in the district
was the Queen's Head, at Keswick, in old John Frank's time.
Buried alive at Oswestry, that man's retirement is a positive loss to tourists—but may he with his kindly family
long live to reap their well-earned *otium cum dignitate.* Such
tenants command success. They combine all the essentials of
the Boniface and Barleycorn families, which may be summed
up in scrupulous attention to the outer and the inner man,
with the clever tact of making their guests, whatever their
condition, thoroughly comfortable and contented. As Montgomery says :—

> " Hail to the timely welcome of an inn ;
> Hail to the room where home and cheer begin :
> Where all the frost-bound feelings melt away,
> And soul-warm sympathies begin to play,
> While independence shows her manly mien,
> And sterling traits of human life are seen."

At Kirkby Stephen there was the inevitable poet Close, with
his interminable books and papers, the latter of which he will
supply whether one asks or no. Poor man, he boasts the
patronage of the Queen and Prince, the French Emperor,
Bishops by the basketful, Duchesses by the dozen, and Peers
innumerable. Whether from a typographical error or no, by
way of a joke indicative of the merits of his authorship or
otherwise, I cannot determine, but he makes out the Hon. Col.
Lowther, M.P., to be the wise man of Stainmore, and has the
advantage of the countenance even of the High Sheriff of Westmoreland and the influential Pease family ! All this is in print,
and much more ; but, knowing the facts, the climax is worth
quotation, and defies criticism :—

" A curious Sight to see at the Kirkby-Stephen Station—the
Poet who has fought so many Battles with Punch ; a Pension
granted by Lord Palmerston, and £100 from the Queen—to see
this man selling his own Books and Portraits at the said Station,
talking with Lords and Bishops. Punch has been pleased to
praise his last book in connection with the talented Martin
Tupper."

· We all three got on talking about dogs and horses, riding and
walking. For the latter exercise I know no better preparation
than four ounces of clarified white soap, four ounces of clarified
mutton suet, and the same quantity of olive oil, with a little
essential oil of lavender, to make the application pleasant. Of
these ingredients mix the three latter, adding the former,
and with the compound anoint your feet well each morning
before going out, and slightly on coming in. So far as I am
concerned, soaping the socks is all that is necessary for hard
and continuous work ; but mentioning this the other day to
Charles Elson, the Northampton pedestrian, who does 56 miles
a day continuously with ease, and will back himself to surpass
his trainer, Mountjoy, who accomplished no less than 60 for
six successive days in the year 1840, he told me all he used was
strong brine at night, and a good dry rub after each journey.
It is wonderful to see that man run, or rather bound, and
spring as he does, without touching the ground with his heel ;
taking a fresh man every mile, and beating ten of them within

the hour. He is only 30 years of age and looks younger, stands
5 feet 5 inches, and has the most delicately small arms to
extraordinary legs, while his chest, of course, is well formed.
But for all foot exercise a vast deal depends on boots.' He, to
be sure, uses shoes; but for each it is essential to have good
dubbing, and perhaps one of the best receipts is this :—Stew
for four hours in a steam bath, and then stir till cold, a pint
of boiled drying oil, the like quantity of neat's-foot oil, one
pound of Russian tallow, half a pound of bees-wax, and the
same weight of Venice turpentine. If the mixture is too stiff
or inconveniently thick, add more neat's-foot oil, and boil
again for a few minutes. For a common dressing for fishing
boots there is nothing like fine shreds of Indian rubber dissolved
in an equal weight of linseed or fish oil or goose grease. These
are of course merely for keeping them in order ; but before every
season, if your man is not up to it, the shoemaker should have
your boots, and thoroughly soak and soften them for at least
three days. Everything depends upon the condition of one's
feet, otherwise the best man in England would be nothing on the
road or moor.

In these papers nothing in the form of a guide-book, of which
there are already sufficient, has been attempted. They have been
written more with a view to forming a grateful *souvenir* of
six happy days passed by friends in the enjoyment of each other's
society ; but the Counties embraced in the narrative are so interesting that a reference to the books consulted may perhaps lead
others to tread the same ground.   The history of Westmoreland
and Cumberland, published in 1829 by Parson and White ; Turner's history of the Anglo-Saxons ; Gibbon's " Decline and Fall ;"
the Rev. Isaac Taylor's " Words and Places," issued this year,
and reviewed in the July number of the *Quarterly*, occur to me
at this moment, as well as " Buckle's History of Civilization,"
to my mind the most interesting and instructive book of this
century ; Magna Britannia et Hibernia, antiqua et nova — a
very scarce and old book by " an impartial hand," but without
the author's name ; Whellan's clear and comprehensive History
and Topography of Cumberland and Westmorland ; Camden's
Britannia ; Lord Dufferin's Letters from High Latitudes ;
Latham's Ethnology of the British Islands ; his Eastern Origin
of Celtic Nations, and his English Language ; Lyell's Antiquity
of Man ; Thos. Wright's the Celt, the Roman, and the Saxon —
a very useful book ; Yonge's History of Christian names ;
Borrow's Wild Wales ; Celtic researches into the origin, traditions, and language of the antient Britons, by Edwd. Davis ;
and Lord Ellesmere's Archœology ; but above all perhaps the
most useful authors for the subject, in a local point of view,
are Ferguson, Anderson, and Worsaac already mentioned.

APPENDICES.

Vide p. 6 ante.

After a similar fashion to the extraordinary mode of courtship referred to—ancient customs, no doubt, for securing a material guarantee for the future prospect of peopling the earth—we have the bundling of Wales, and the nocturnal visits of the betrothed in the Canton of Unterwald. The publication of the remarks, circumstances, observations, and facts I felt compelled to notice with reference to the preponderance of illegitimate births in Cumberland having startled a number of persons possibly, and "nettled" an anonymous correspondent writing under the sobriquet of "A Cumbrian." It is, perhaps, better to extract the note from Anderson's Cumberland ballads, referred to in the text under the date of the 17th May, premising that no more fair or truthful writer is extant:

Note III., p. 202.

"When aw t'auld fwok were liggin asleep.

A Cumbrian peasant pays his addresses to his sweetheart during the silence and solemnity of midnight, when every bosom is at rest save that of love and sorrow. Anticipating her kindness, he will travel ten or twelve miles over hills, bogs, moors, and mosses, undiscouraged by the length of the road, the darkness of the night, or the intemperature of the weather. On reaching her habitation he gives a gentle tap at the window of her chamber, at which signal she immediately arises, dresses herself, and proceeds with all possible silence to the door, which she gently opens, lest a creaking hinge or a barking dog should awaken the family. On his entrance into the kitchen, the luxuries of a Cumbrian cottage —cream and sugared curds—are placed before him by the fair hand of his Dulcinea. Next the courtship commences, previously to which the fire is darkened or extinguished, lest its light should guide to the window some idle or licentious eye. In this dark and uncomfortable situation (at least uncomfortable to all but lovers) they remain till the advance of day, depositing in each other's bosoms the secrets of love, and making vows of unalterable affection. Though I am so far partial to my fair countrywomen—deaf in some instances—and respect their very prejudices, I cannot conclude this note without representing to them the danger and impropriety of admitting the visits of their lovers during these hours of the night, which virtue and innocence have appropriated to repose. Nothing more encourages unbecoming familiarities, nothing more promotes dissolute manners, nothing more endangers female chastity, nothing more facilitates the designs of the seducer

than these *night courtships*. A custom that leads to such serious
consequences, however general it may be, or whatever antiquity it
may claim, cannot be too soon abolished ; and I am so much convinced of the good sense and purity of mind of the Cumbrian fair,
that I am confident as soon as they reflect on the guilt and misery
to which it so often leads, their virtue will take alarm, and they
will see the danger which arises from admitting the visits of men
in improper situations and at improper times."

This custom, and the statute fairs still prevailing, cause and
effect being indissoluble, and human nature as it was in the
beginning, I have nothing to retract—nay, rather much to add,
were it worth while, on this subject, and that of ignorance and
superstition. Suffice it to say, however, the Cockermouth,
Keswick, and Penrith Railway will be opened next month—the
Directors having exercised in these days of carelessness and
costs a wise discretion in their cautious delay—and civilization
is at hand. While yielding to no one in loving the Lake District, with its every yard of beauty and of interest, so readily
enjoyed on horseback, with a knapsack or otherwise, it would
be stupid to ignore facts—such blindness is mere prejudice,
and concealment weakness, if not worse.

Let any impartial man read Miss Martineau's little guide
book, and peruse pages 35-8 and 57 if he denies the intellectual condition of the county, which, existing in this enlightened
age, when reason guides the chariot, bearing onward, swiftly onward, science and knowledge understanded of the people, shames
to one's very face the pious frauds spoken of by Matthew Paris,
the most eminent historiau of the thirteenth century ; Tubin-
gen's deluge and Auriol's Ark at Toulouse in 1524 ; Horst's
golden tooth in 1595 ; giants 30 feet high, winged dragons and
armies flying through the air, all implicitly believed in with
other falsehoods no less extravagant and more crafty during the
Ages of Faith, which were really cycles of delusion and darkness.

P. 18 ante.

With reference to the holmgang, the reader may be referred
to the 12th sect. of Worsaae's book, as well as other authors
mentioned ; and for its illustration to No. 542 in this year's
academy, "A Norwegian duel," by Tidemand, which claimed
as prominent attention during the season as any work in the
gallery. Until the Exhibition of 1862 this great artist, the
head of his school, was almost unknown in this country, save
to the highest connoisseurs in art, such as the late Duke of
Hamilton, the late Lord Lansdowne, the late Lord Ellesmere,
and Messrs Cowan and Mathiesen, each of whom lent his pictures
on that memorable occasion. Mr Phillips, of 23, Cockspur-
street, London, in making his extraordinary acquisitions in
1862, all of which were particularised in my "Impression"
under the date the 28th November in that year, selected at
once from this artist the only picture exhibited on sale, No.
1428, and no one who beheld "The Administration of the
Sacrament to sick persons and cripples in a Norwegian hut,"
can ever forget its force, or dispute the accurate taste dictating
its purchase. But he did more, for he at once commissioned
the artist to paint an original picture, leaving the size and
detail and subject and everything to himself. The result is the

51

remarkable work contributed. I make no apology in explaining it in the artist's own words, feeling assured that in an historical point of view it will be as interesting as the painting itself is in an artistic. So soon as the letter reached England, the following literal translation was placed in my hands :—

"You have asked me for some explanatory remarks on my picture of "A Norwegian Duel," and I have much pleasure in noting down the following facts and observations :—There are traditions, songs, and legends of such fights, which generally occurred at weddings, wakes, and yule feasts; in short, whenever and wherever there were gatherings of the people. On such occasions grudges, enmities, and rancours came to a head, and were settled by combat; or—and such an event is suggested by my picture—the dispute was caused by some incident which occurred at the feast, when brains and tongue were excited with drink, and the provocation thus given had to be atoned for in blood. These combats, as compared to the brawls of the present day, were decent, solemn, and in fact, chivalrous. They had their rules, which every one observed, and which were enforced by the bystanders. Their issue was held as a legal decision. Few complaints arising from such deeds were ever made to the authorities; but in most cases, more especially when no mortal blows had been struck, some sort of compensation or indemnity was agreed on by the families of the combatants. I, myself, know of a case where a man's arm was wrenched out of the socket in the course of a fight. Instead of an action for assault, the case was arbitrated on by the friends of both parties, and the compensation consisted in a few days' assistance in harvesting, which the victor promised to give to the man he had injured. The duel which forms the subject of my picture is a fight with axes—a weapon much in use about 150 years ago. It is still found in some of the peasants' houses, and fine specimens are preserved in the Old Norwegian Museum at Christiania. The axe was the peasant's staff and weapon, which he carried about wherever he went, even to church, when they were placed in the porch, which to this day retains its old name of the armoury. The handle was bent and shod with iron stripes, to guard it from blows; and the blade was thin and carefully worked. My picture represents the issue of a combat with this weapon, and that issue—in the present instance—is fatal to both combatants. According to tradition, the duel took place at a farm in Tellemark, in Southern Norway, and the place is still shown where seven men fell in combat. They had long been feasting and drinking at the farm, when high words were uttered, closely followed by defiance, and that by fight. The man who had first been struck down has been laid on a bench near the table. His young wife, frantic with grief, leans over him, and her child, dimly conscious of a great misfortune, hides its face in the mother's lap. Next to her a little boy, roused from sleep, climbs upon a chair. An elderly man—one who has seen many blows struck in his time—leans over the body, and, hoping against hope, examines the wound. The other combatant has meanwhile been raised by his friends. Between the two groups an old woman —the mother of the dead man—presses forward; on her arm is a winding-sheet, which women frequently took to feasts, so as to be prepared for all emergencies. Grief, wrath, and revenge strive for the mastery, and with her left arm raised, she invokes heaven's curse upon the murderer. The whole party has broken up—the women move the plates and dishes. In the background, a young man leaps over the table to join the principal group, resume the quarrel, and perhaps renew the fight. Crowded together near the hearth, and struggling, illuminated by its blaze, are some women and children. From the bench this side the hearth rises an old blind fiddler, and attempts to grope his way to the door. Two children have sought refuge in the bed, where, frantic with fear,

n

they cling to one another. Quite in the foreground to the right, a man comes up from the cellar with a can of beer. The farm-house is built in the oldest fashion to be found in Norway. There is no chimney, and the smoke eddies up and escapes through an outlet in the roof. A moveable bracket projecting over the hearth serves for the hanging up of the pots and kettles over the fire. It is ornamented with a dragon's head, and this ornamentation, too, in a manner, connects the present with the old pagan times.—With very best greetings, ADOLPH TIDEMAND.

Mr Alfred Morrison, of Fonthill Abbey, a munificent patron of art, secured this interesting example of the Scandinavian school, the size of which is 7ft. 9½in. by 5ft. 6¾in. sight measure.

With reference to my friend Mr Phillips, I wrote the following paragraph for the *Durham Chronicle* of the 15th January last :—" In our issues of the 10th of October and 28th of November, 1862, in the series of papers on the International Exhibition of that year, occasion was taken to review, amongst the many collections then exhibited with an emulation and success never surpassed, that of Mr Robert Phillips, of 23, Cockspur-street, Charing Cross, goldsmith, by appointment, to H.R.H. the Prince of Wales. It is unnecessary to repeat the high opinion then expressed of him, either as a virtuoso or a jeweller. At that time his reproductions and adaptations to the present fashion of Egyptian and Etruscan ornaments elicited the unanimous applause of the best judges, and bore the palm even against Castellani, while his display of coral surpassed all the Italian courts unitedly could show. In full corroboration of every word the writer said, the subsequent report to the Imperial Government of the members of the French section of the International Jury upon the entirety of the Exposition, published under the immediate direction of their chief, M. Michel Chevalier, vol. 16, p. 45, observes :—' M. Phillips, de Londres, est un concurrent sérieux pour nos fabricants ; sa collection de coiffures en corail est remarquable par l'heureux ajustement des formes et la beauté des couleurs. Ses bijoux, dans le genre antique, et entre autres, plusiers colliers dans le goût toscan, sont de véritables types de grâce.' At the establishment in Cockspur-street has been for some days on view a marvellous collection of the finest coral and works of art—for such Phillips' jewels are rather than mere displays of wealth, gems in them, wondrous specimens though they be, being auxiliary and subservient to the general effect. Going with the times, no sooner was the Danish marriage with our English Prince—now the fresh occasion of happy auspices—decided upon, than, in addition to the adaptations previously mentioned, he ransacked Scandinavian models, and has produced a variety of interesting objects in the most correct taste and perfect workmanship, all from antique designs, though new to our English ideas. Nor are Russian articles, which attracted so much attention in 1862, wanting ; and all these things are so well executed, from table plate up to personal ornaments, as to rank as works of art each one of them. In our issue, 31st October, 1862, the sixth of the papers above-mentioned, Mosaic work was specially entered into, and one of the most beautiful objects in Mr Phillips' present display is a specimen of Russian *pietra dura*, representing a cluster of various fruits, executed in the round. The raspberries are carved out of rhodonite, the brambles are amethysts, the currants cornelians, the cherries carbuncles, and the foliage jade. By such means is this mockery of nature produced, and the illusion to the eye is so exquisite, that the palate or the touch can alone test the imposture. Among his acquisitions from the great Exhibition were a set of nine miniature enamels, forming *plaques* for a casket, by M. Charles Lepec; and these little gems, which we have had frequent opportunities of examining at leisure, at once stamp the artist as without any question the most original and consummate the world has ever seen. Petitot, Zincke, Toutin, W. Craft, and numbers of others, brilliant and soft as are their examples, all were copyists, but this man is purely original, not only in design—perhaps a more perfect draughtsman never existed—but in his mode of treatment. As a climax to his efforts in 1862, Mr Phillips shows the greatest work Lepec has yet conceived or executed, and perhaps the finest specimen of enamel extant. The object is a tazza, or some might call it a *coupe.* In the hollow is a picture—classic in conception, minutely delicate in detail, and equally brilliant and harmonious in color, as seems invariably to be the case with him—representing Venus swiftly gliding over the surface of the sea in a car drawn by mermaids, while overhead hovers in mid-air Cupid, with a torch in one hand, and in the other the silken reins wherewith he laughing gently guides the water nymphs. The mermaids represent the two different types of beauty, the blonde and the brunette ; and in each figure there is so much female loveliness, both of form and expression, that one cannot forbear lamenting the hard condition of mythology which dooms a termination so ignoble to beings at once so attractive and fascinating in the outset of their career :— *Superne formosa mulier, desinit in piscem.* The half-buoyant figure of Venus, who, with her fair tresses falling over her shoulders in glossy luxuriance, and her snowy scarf floating gaily in the summer breeze, seems scarce to touch the car, but looks as if about to soar on high, is full of exquisite grace and joyous *abandon.* The gentle swell and crisp ripple of the sea, upon whose blue water the moon sheds her lustre, is charmingly expressed, as also the serene aspect of the sky—its azure vault studded with golden stars and dappled with silver clouds. In the rim, which is concave, are medallion miniatures, marvellously painted, of some of the most celebrated women, who, whether in the records of historic or imaginative literature, have exercised the most potent influence over ' the lords of creation.' Of this number are Delilah, Omphale, Semiramide, Armida, Cleopatra, and Desdemona, whose portraits are in every instance surrounded with allegorical devices emblematic of their respective characters. On the foot, which, as well as the stem of the cup, is profusely decorated, are pictures of Laura, Beatrice, and Leonora, the heroines of the three great Italian poets. The outside of the tazza is elaborately ornamented with flowers and foliage, painted in a manner to resemble the lacquer-work of the Japanese. It is not our intention to write any dissertation upon the various merits of the *cloisonné* or *champlevé* processes·· the works of Cellini, those of Venice, Flanders, Florence, or Limoges ; but we believe that so rare an object of fine art of its kind as that we have attempted thus imperfectly to describe, has not been seen in any age, and the sensation it has created can be no matter of surprise. At the Exhibition of 1862 a medal, No. 6,658, class 33, was awarded to Mr Phillips for ' works in gold and silver, coral and precious stones, excellence of design and manufacture,' and no one has better sustained his reputation."

Mr Morrison also became the shrewd purchaser of this marvellous object, of the *plaques* mentioned above, many other of the choicest gems in the Exhibition, and I hope may secure those with which M. Lepec has just supplied my friend, about whom the *Art Journal* writes this month :—

THE POMPEIAN NARCISSUS.

The agents of the government excavating at Pompeii, under Signor Fiorelli, have recently discovered some relics of great beauty and value, of which one of the most precious is a statuette of Narcissus, to which, in its sacred oxide of nearly eighteen centuries, a place has been assigned in the Museo Borbonico at Naples, among the bronzes from Herculaneum, Pompeii, and Stabiæ. Our knowledge of the statuette is derived from a reproduction in the possession of Mr Phillips, 23 Cockspur-street, who has been appointed the agent in this country for the disposal of copies. The height of the figure is about two feet ; it stands with the weight of the body resting on the left leg, the right leg behind, as if having either suddenly stopped, or moving very stealthily forward. The right hand is held out as the action of a listener enjoying silence, and the inclination of the head forward and sideways coincides with the hand, as the natural position assumed by a person either listening to an indistinct sound, or waiting for its repetition. The left hand rests upon the side, with the elbow thrown out. The hair is confined by a chaplet without leaves, but with bunches of berries over the forehead—perhaps myrtle or ivy, in which case the artist must have intended a convivial crown. From the left shoulder depend the spoils of a goat, in allusion to the hunting excursions undertaken with his sister. Another reference to this is the Cothurnus, which is admirable in design, as from the heel-piece rises a flower that spreads forward on every practicable space to the front of the foot. The modelling of this, together with the front lacing, is most perfect, and the same care prevails in another part yet more difficult, that is the hair, the arrangement and working of which show the most refined taste and masterly skill. He may be supposed to be listening to the love-wailing of the despised Echo, or he may be contemplating his own figure in the pool, and approaching it with a silent and stealthy step. Youth and beauty are as definite in the figure as in the Apollino, and, although at rest, it is as light as the Mercury of Gian Bologna. In the face there is an individuality far apart from the grave majesty of the Greek type. The expression brings us back to the idea of the wailing Echo ; the voice seems to be behind him, and he refuses to turn. Whether we consider the back or the front, the course of the lines swelling and receding is remarkably beautiful, and the easy quietude and wrapt attention of the attitude take us into the story, without leading us to forget the figure, to which, indeed, it is something to have given a living consciousness of superior personal attraction with some affectation and a maintenance of the style known among ourselves as *dandyism*. The manner and feeling of the work seems to be Roman. By the way, of Mr Philips's statuette as a copy, it must be said that nothing can be more perfect—we speak, of course, of the surface imitation of the figure, not having seen the original.

P. 37, ante.

Without an acquaintance with the facts the song loses half its point, but the performance consisted of the trial scene from "the Merchant of Venice," and Bottom's dream in the "Midsummer's Night's Dream." The verse quoted in the text was the third, the rest being.

Gloomily roll'd the dull world along
Till Pierus gave birth to the Muses and Song ;
But Joy ask'd for more than the Grecian Nine,
So Noah bethought him, and plated the Vine.
Chorus.

The first of toasts on our list must be,
"The Island Queen !" with three time three !
May guardian angels round her smile,
And shield the throne of the sea girt isle !
Chorus.

* * * * *

Now we'll drink in dark red wine,
"The Tragic Muse in her wreath of vine !"
And then a goblet full I'll ask
For "Thalia with her comic mask."
Chorus.

With reverend mien we now will fill
A bumper to our own "Sweet Will !"
Accept, Great Shade ! our widow's mite,
Poor tribute that we bring to-night.
Chorus.

Toast now our Actors, every one ;—
Thanks for tragedy, thanks for fun,
Thanks for song, and thanks for scene,
Thanks for the Duke, the King, the Queen.
Chorus.

Thanks for saving Antonio's life
From bloody Shylock's sharpen'd knife,
Thanks to the Clowns so ably led
By wit, for once, in an ass's head.
Chorus.

Thanks to our friend, that *rara-aris*,
Gratiano and Quince, as joined in Davis,
Bassanio, too, who has to try-on
The tawny skin of a roaring lion.
Chorus.

Thank the "Clerk" that a "tinker" made,
The bearded youth that Thisbe played ;
Thank the bright elves and fairy myths,
Phipps, Wetherell, Bell, and little Smiths.
Chorus.

Thank Starveling, he who next appears,
Knight of the thimble and the shears.
Starveling ! give to thy starving truce,
Forswear thy cabbage and cook thy goose.
Chorus.

Thanks to our friend who fills the chair,
Whose generous hand and vértû rare ;
Whose gems and counsels, lace and gold,
Made *our* Venetians outshine the old.
Chorus.

Time fails to follow the tempting theme !
Venice farewell ! farewell, sweet "Dream !"
Good bye ! sweet Bottom, Titania, Puck ;
Adieu, ye flowers, where bees do suck !
Chorus.

Adieu, proud plumes, gold lace, and pearls ;
Adieu "mechanical," ill-dressed churls ;
Adieu the Duke, the Court, the Courtier,
The rascal Jew, and the learned Portia.
Chorus.

Adieu the band, the tuneful choir,
The painter's brush, and Marshall's lyre ;
The curtain falls—dimm'd is the light.
"Good night ! with lullaby—Good night !"
Chorus.

And may no sorrow here be found,
But mirth and laughter, toasts go round.
"Tho' last, not least in our esteem"—
Tom Speciall's health —thanks for his theme.
Chorus.

———

It seems a strange thing after all, when one comes to think about it, that there should have been so much hubbub and fuss throughout the breadth of merrie England and all Germany to celebrate the birthday of a child 300 years ago, and that even villages became inspired by the enthusiasm and excitement of the moment. The rector of Haughton-le-Skerne, the Rev. Edward Cheese, though highly and emphatically disapproving of the stage and all connected with it, as leading too likely towards dissipation and neglect of work among his parishioners, strove as hard as any man to get up in the neighbouring town of Darlington a pronunciation of a more permanent and important character than it was found possible to achieve, hit upon the happy expedient of localising the celebration of the 23rd of April, 1864, in "the old tithe barn" attached to the rectory, which he of all incumbents on record has made the place of genial gatherings. The apartment was hung with flags ; at the back of the dais or stage at the north end was placed the initials of the immortal bard in coloured lamps, and the audience filled the whole of the available space left. About seven o'clock, he read a short address, and introduced the name of Mr J. G. Grant, whom he had specially brought over to lecture on " the Life and Works of Shakspeare." The proceedings, however, commenced with a performance by Mrs Cheese on the pianoforte, and then Mr Grant stepped forward. As a lecturer generally, and on Shakspeare in particular, this gentleman has few equals. Perhaps his reading of plays and his wonderful power of expression are without parallel in the North of England. He said the bard of Avon had composed something like thirty-six distinct works, and among them six or seven tragedies, the least excellent of which were superior to all except the highest order of the Greek drama, while four of them—Macbeth, Othello, Hamlet, and Lear—infinitely

surpassed all tragedies, whether ancient or modern, Greek or
Gothic. His comedies, such as "As You Like It," "Much
Ado about Nothing," "Two Gentlemen of Verona," and
"Twelfth Night," literally overflowed with wit and humour,
besides abounding with profound philosophy and exquisite
poetry. His romantic dramas, such as "The Tempest" and
"A Midsummer Night's Dream," with the spirits and monsters
in the former, and elves and fairies in the latter, exemplify in
the highest degree the marvellous inventive faculty of the poet's
art—being the pure creation of his original and versatile genius.
Indeed, as Dr. Johnson observed, had such beings been possible
in life, they would have acted, and thought, and spoken, and
moved precisely as Shakspeare tells us, so natural is he even
in the preternatural. The lecturer's description of Ariel was
charming—"light, graceful, humane, joyous, and exquisite,
one of those

> ' Gay creatures of the elements
> That in the colours of the rainbow live,
> And play on plighted clouds.'

The very essence of ethereality ! The very impersonation of
glancing, darting, glittering, and unsubstantial beauty and of
thought, like the rapidity of motion ! Almost too delicate and
fragile to be other than feminine, and yet not female." Shakspeare's historical dramas, the lecturer remarked, were equally
admirable in poetry and natural in spirit. Great kings, grasping and stormy barons, sturdy yeomen, and crafty priests being
alike faithfully pourtrayed. One grand peculiarity of Shakspeare
was this, that his manner was without mannerism, his style
ever without conceit ; and whether he dwelt upon town life or
country, legal or medical experience, the court, the camp, or the
council, in each he excelled. So profoundly proficient was his
knowledge, that his writings never evinced any ignorance of
detail or acquisition, the want of which was so marvellous.
His lyrics and sonnets –" Venus and Adonis" and "the Rape
of Lucrece," for instance—were full of grace and beauty ; and
all his writings classed together formed an aggregate of intellectual power and wealth unequalled and unapproached in the
purest sphere of literature and art of any age or of any country, proving line by line and book after book his inexhaustible
acquaintance with human nature, and applying to himself
what he wrote of gorgeous Cleopatra—

> "Age cannot wither,
> Nor custom stale, his infinite variety."

By way of illustrating poetic fancy, Mr Grant read, as only he
can read, the scene between Prospero and Ariel. As an instance
of the sublime power of the poet, he gave that grand and
dramatic scene in Richard III.—Clarence's dream. Comedy
was illustrated by the dialogue, graceful and humourous, from
"As You Like It," between Orlando and Rosalind, she dis-
guised as a boy, and pretending to act his Rosalind, besides
the brilliant squabble between Benedict and Beatrice, in
"Much ado about Nothing," in a manner which delighted the
audience. In defending the morality of Shakespeare, the lecturer observed that it would be unfair to try the age of Elizabeth by that of Victoria ; great allowance ought to be made
for the bold rudeness of his age, compared with the squeamish

and almost morbid sentimental delicacy of our own. Even his lightest dramas, with all their faults, were openly acted before "the virgin Queen" and her "virgin court" without one word being omitted by the actors, or one syllable of disapprobation from the audience. Such might be the errors of the age, but he mentioned these facts in justification of the idol of the day. As an example of his moral and religious power, Mr Grant read with wonderful expression, from Henry V., the King's conversation with two sentinels of his army the night before the battle of Agincourt. Surely, he said, a man who in his own age and by his own contemporaries was called commonly "brave Will," "kind," "sweet," "gentle Will Shakspeare," and in whose honour pretty flowers are named to this day "Sweet William," could not have been any other than one claiming our tenderest affection and our deepest respect, both for his moral excellence and his unbounded talent. At different parts of the lecture, Mr Grant called upon the rustic choral society to perform "Full fathoms five," "Where the bee sucks," and "Come unto these yellow sands," from the Tempest, and "Who is Sylvia" (Cymbeline), and each was given in a manner and with a strength of lungs so vigorous as to show the extreme salubrity of the climate, if nothing else, and in a dialect purely local. By way of conclusion, "a fairy song" divided a recitation of the quarrel in Julius Cæsar by Messrs Pallister and Brown, representing Brutus and Cassius—and the handkerchief scene from Othello by Messrs Stabler and Boddy, who sustained the characters of the Moor and Iago respectively. These two efforts produced, notwithstanding their serious nature, the most unbounded mirth, so extremely solemn and furious and determined were the hearty volunteers, one of whom wore an immense beard and moustaches as his Roman disguise ! ! The proceedings terminated with complimentary speeches and "God Save the Queen," everybody being convinced that no thought could be happier than that of enlisting the sympathies and securing the services of the natives in an entertainment for such a purpose, thus eliciting their interest with a lecture so admirable in every way as that, by the kindness of the Rector, they had the good fortune to attend.

In the year 1852, I witnessed, both at Devonshire House and the Lyceum in Sunderland, the performance of that rare band of amateurs who laid the foundation of the guild of literature and art. Antiquated fossil playgoers, carping, snarling critics, who spurn the very notion of non-professional attempts as something impertinent and audacious, were alike astonished and bewitched. Under the sole direction of Charles Dickens —than whom no better or more life-like actor treads the stage —Mark Lemon, poor Augustus Egg, Frank Stone, Charles Knight, Peter Cunningham, Robert Bell, Wilkie Collins, great John Tenniel, F. W. Topham, and others, formed the troupe for whom Lytton Bulwer wrote "Not so bad as we seem," and dear old Clarkson Stanfield, Telbin, Pitt, Louis Haghe, and glowing David Roberts painted. Such a galaxy of talent defied criticism, and achieved a success that is remembered by each witness of it as nothing short of perfection. To attempt anything beyond *tableaux vivants* or charades in the way of acting, requires a combination of talent and tact at all times difficult

to attain; but the very thought of such a thing in Darlington,
of all places in the three kingdoms, was considered by many
hopeless, and wicked by not a few. So much for faint-hearted-
ness and spurious piety, whose professors never reckoned so
much without their host as on Tuesday, the 26th of April,
when the Darlington Amateur Dramatic Club celebrated the
Tercentenary. The entertainment provided by the committee
even exceeded the most sanguine anticipations of their best
friends—so thoroughly well done was every detail. The names
of these gentlemen should be recorded, and each thanked—the
chairman, Mr Edward Pease Elgee; his coadjutors, Messrs
Bailey, Heaviside, C. Brady, J. Hoggett, T. Brunton, J. B.
Kirsop, J. Davis, W. Lear, J. Fenwick, W. Lee, M. Frier,
Thomas Potts, and James Wilson; the dramatic directors,
Messrs W. A. Smith, T. Swinburne, and J. K. Wilkes; the
manager, Mr James Kendall; the costume director, Mr M.
Barker; the courteous and indefatigable hon. sec., Mr G. B.
Carter; the artists, Messrs Elton, Kendall, Bell, and John
Dinsdale; and, "though last not least in our esteem," Mr
Clapham and his assistant, Mr Walker (by whom "the fairies"
were allowed to aid with charming effect, and no girls could
have looked or done better than these clever school-boys)—one
and all deserve the kindest greeting. For some days before
the performance tickets were so enquired after that it was a
matter of no surprise numbers were refused admittance, and
the Central Hall has perhaps never witnessed a superior or
more universally gratified audience. The little theatre, a trifle
too little, with its elegant proscenium surmounted by the arms
and monogram of Shakspeare, was arranged on the platform,
and the apartment so judiciously lighted that the stage, as in
Italy, became, as it ought to be, the centre of attraction. Before half-past seven o'clock every available space seemed filled,
and there could not be less than 700 present. Precisely at
that hour the bell tinkled—here, it may be observed, nothing
could exceed throughout the evening the punctual attention to
stage management, it far exceeded the ordinary accuracy of
more pretentious houses—and up went the green curtain, dis-
playing Mr Elton's graceful drop-scene (fairies dancing on the
yellow sands in glowing moonlight), which was much applauded.
The performance then commenced with the overture to Cas-
sandra by the Philharmonic band, who occupied the orchestra.
At its conclusion an admirably painted street scene in Venice,
executed by Messrs Bell and Dinsdale from a drawing of Mr
Elton's on the spot, was disclosed; and Mr Kendall delivered
the following prologue, which he had composed expressly for
the occasion, and by nothing could the earnest of the treat in
store have been better harbingered :—

> " All the world's a stage :
> And all the men and women merely players,
> They have their exits and their entrances."

> Three hundred years ago the world beheld
> An entrance rare. His life was gentle,
> And the elements so mixed in him
> That nature might stand up
> And say to all the world, "This is a man !"

Three hundred years ago none thought the babe
Slumbering in his cradle should rise up
And strike with wondrous hand a harp whose chords
Responding nature over echoes back,
Above the noise of party, sect, or creed.
Strange! that as lengthening time piles up the years,
And generations pass, and science grows,
His words but gather force, and meaning too :
And furnish cottage, palace, senate, hall,
With maxim, proverb, wit, law, rhetoric !
Hail, William Shakspeare ! such a fame is thine,
That statues, monuments will fall to dust
While still the English drama lives in thee :
And lives because of thee : and with new life
Must live, since thou hast lived, tho' now and then,
And here and there, men sagely think to do
Both God and man a service, when they give
A dubious hint, or silly slanderous sneer—
To deprecate the drama, which as surely,
So long as man shall " strut and fret his hour
Upon this earthly stage," will ever " hold
The mirror up to nature," to present
A reflex of the manners and the ways of men.
Friends, fellow-men ! let no apology
Be needed for the play. Apology?
T'would be apologising to the world
That Shakspeare lived ! The drama follows man
As surely as his shadow. "Look you to't"
No queer or ugly traits of character
Of *yours* get photographed ;—why then of course
You'll say " how wicked !"—then perchance you'll try
To break " the mirror," " drink up Easil?" ha !
Or " eat a crocodile ?" " Odds bodikins"
" You may as well go stand upon the beach
And bid the main flood bate his usual height,"
As seek to still those plaudits which resound
Along the shores of time—whose voices cry
" Here was a Cæsar, when comes such another ?"
Three centuries ago he lived, and spoke,
And, tho' thus long his presence has departed,
His spirit walks among the sons of men,
Majestic as the forms of life his pen awoke,
But with far statelier tread.
" Why man ? He doth bestride the narrow world
Like a Colossus, and we petty men
Walk under his huge shade, and peep about
To find our little graves."

Ladies and Gentlemen,—While to-night Darlington presents
her humble quota to swell the mighty meed of those large honours
to which the name of William Shakspeare is entitled, we ask you
to be somewhat less critical of the performance than considerate
of the occasion that prompts the attempt. Hear us for our
cause—believe us for the sincerity of our tribute ; censure us with
a wisdom that separates not too distinctly between the will and
the deed. Say not with Polonius, " I will use them after their
deserts"—but, with Hamlet, resolve, both for your own tranquillity
and our [comfort, " Much better." " Use every man after his
deserts, and who should escape whipping ?" " Use us therefore after
the honour of the occasion ; the less we deserve the more is in
your bounty."

Discriminating applause marked the most striking passages,
and the audience at once settled down, with the assurance of a
foregone conclusion as to the merits of the company by this

worthy specimen of one of its most active and able members, to peruse

THE PROGRAMME.

GLEE—"Blow, blow, thou wintry wind."
Members of the Choral Society.

SELECTION FROM THE MERCHANT OF VENICE.

Act I., Scene 3.

Scene 1.—GRAND CANAL.

Shylock......Mr M. Barker.   Antonio......Mr M. Frier.
Bassanio......................Mr J. Fenwick.
OVERTURE.........."Massaniello."—*Auber*..............Band.

Act IV.

Scene 2.—COURT OF JUSTICE.

Duke of Venice.................Mr C. Brady.

Shylock..................... .... Mr M. Barker.
Antonio ...Mr M. Frier.   Bassanio....Mr J. Fenwick.
Gratiano....Mr J. Davis.   Salanio....Mr W. Hodgson.
Portia..Mr J. Kendall. Nerissa..Mr Bell. Clerk..Mr G. R. Phipps.

An Interval of Ten Minutes.

OVERTURE..........."Tancredi.".................. Band.
Overture to Midsummer Night's Dream—*Mendelssohn*.. Piano-forte.

Mr J. W. Marshall.

SELECTION FROM A MIDSUMMER NIGHT'S DREAM.

Act I., Scene 2.

Scene 1.—INTERIOR OF QUINCE'S HOUSE.

Quince......Mr J. Davis.   Bottom......Mr J. Kendall.
Snug......Mr J. Fenwick   Flute......Mr W. Hodgson.
Snout....Mr G. R. Phipps.   Starveling....Mr H. Cuthbertson.
Song............"Where the Bee sucks.".........Miss Shutt.
Wedding March ......Mendelssohn.......... Band.

Act II.

Scene 2.—A WOOD NEAR ATHENS.

Puck......Mr W. Bell   Oberon......Master H. Wetherell.
Titania..............Master A. Pile.
Mustard-seed.. ....⎫   ⎧............ Master O. Smith.
Cobweb .... ⎬Fairies⎨............ „   B. Smith.
Peas-blossom.........⎭   ⎩............ „   J. Phipps.
Duct......" I know a Bank"......Miss Shutt & Mr Jas. Wilson.

Scene 2.—A WOOD NEAR ATHENS.

Glee................."Ye Spotted Snakes"............Choir.

Scene 4.—INTERIOR OF QUINCE'S HOUSE.

Finale........................National Anthem.

Even without the graceful supplication of Mr Kendall, it would be an ungenial and shabby part to criticise an amateur performance—but the finished execution of every portion of this varied programme forbids it. With the most vivid and refreshing memory of the brilliant representations of the distinguished artists previously mentioned, let me award advisedly the most unqualified applause to this local effort, and say the great event of this year's April has been celebrated in a manner appropriate to the occasion. The dresses were excellent, and in the best taste. No one over-acted his part, or missed his cue. Each looked his character and observed his bye-play. To say this of Shylock, The Duke, Antonio, Gratiano, is no mean praise ; yet 'tis true. In the measured calm of Portia, no one on earth could recognise "bully Bottom ;" nor in the jewelled exquisite, elegant Bassanio, that stupid dunder-head "Snug the Joiner;" while the metamorphose of the observant "Clerk" into that imbecile coward, "Snout the Tinker," was as preposterous and complete as good acting could accomplish. The characters were so well sustained that none other of the company could so well have taken his neighbour's part. Titania, with her clear voice, was charming; and perhaps one of the most telling scenes was that in which she lies watching her drowsy swain, the choir concealed singing the while, "Ye Spotted Snakes." Puck was as mischievous and agile, and as graceful as he ought to be, which is saying a good deal—indeed how he managed to cut so many capers was marvellous to behold. Oberon, and the smaller fairies, "Masters" Cobweb, Mustard-seed, and Peas-blossom, could not have been better; nor could the ass's head or its management have been exceeded by the live animal. The whole performance was admirable; dignity and drollery, delicious music and beautiful scenery, combined to make it most enjoyable. When one considers that all these gentlemen, with the exception of Mr Barker, have never appeared in public before, the completeness of the arrangements and the performance was something surprising. Oddly enough, too, the bulk of them are engaged in the three Banks in the town. Miss Shutt was encored in "Where the bee sucks," and gave in answer to the compliment, "Tell me where is fancy bred." The musical part of the entertainment was unexceptionable, and on more than one occasion the curtain was raised for actors and choir to bow their acknowledgments of the hearty applause they elicited and deserved. The chairman, Mr Elgee, announced, amidst great enthusiasm, that the performance would be repeated the following evening at reduced prices, to accommodate a vast number who had been disappointed, and it transpired that the proceeds would be divided equally amongst the Philharmonic Band as to one-third —another third being placed at the disposal of Mr Marshall, to whom the public owes so much for his education of the musical talent of the place, and by whom it will be applied for that purpose—the remaining third being reserved by the Dramatic Committee for future use.

It should be mentioned that Mr Day, the proprietor of the Theatre in the Green-tree Field, with the kindliest fellow-feeling, suspended his performance on the 26th, and that Mr Garthwaite, the painter and house-decorator, with happy readiness to do a good turn, as his wont is, gratuitously supplied the volunteer artists with all the appliances of which they stood in need. Coming so abruptly upon the great success of the first performance, that of the following evening was by many feared as a venture too hazardous, they said "it would be better to leave well alone." The result, however, was another triumph adding fresh laurels to all concerned, surprising and delighting a house almost as good as that of the previous evening. Touching the audience, it was singular to remark the almost total absence of country families who are in the habit of attending the various entertainments at the Central Hall; theirs was the loss, however, and so many felt when they discovered too late the choice amusement they missed. Instead of failure by repetition, the acting was even better than on the first attempt.

Good as Shylock was then, his bye-play was more subtle on the second occasion—Gratiano and Peter Quince were equally graphic—while Bottom and Snout, the tinker, were, if possible, more irresistibly comic and diverting—indeed, young Mr Phipps kept us all convulsed with laughter whenever he appeared. The poor workhouse bairns had the entire front of the gallery placed at their disposal by the generous thought of the committee, who seem to have left little immaturely or hastily considered, and for whom, with the actors and musicians, the celebration dinner was arranged. Well, they deserved any mark of approbation, and right heartily without a doubt it was given. So far as the pauper children were concerned, however, the hours were prudently considered by the authorities as too late to permit more than the compliment being paid, but the will may be taken for the deed, and the exigency regretted. The actors were photographed of course. "Photographed!" that's no joke at any time, but "a swan on a road" is nothing to the absurd fun of seeing one's own chums "taken in character," which we witnessed in garish daylight, under the agreeable influence of a blighting, fluttering north-east wind and sunshine. Poor old Shylock, with his look of scowling horror, his scales just drop't—the Duke, in all the gorgeous array of rich silk robes, velvet, ermine, and snowy-flowing beard (over his own) —the elegant Bassanio, always gay and jaunty, in black velvet slashed with white satin in diamonds bordered with gold, his jewelled cap and pied plume powdered with pearls—Salanio, in plum velvet, pomona cloak, and gold lace wherever it could increase effect—Antonio, in sad and sober garments, relieved with scarlet, as became his peculiarly unpleasant position— Gratiano, in Mazarin blue velvet and silver—all waiting for that horrid moment "ready," shivering in the open air, so that the stage itself should be included in the negative, formed a group, the like of which we never saw before except at Christmas, and from which, disregarding altogether Portia, Nerissa, and the Clerk, we might have expected, had there been some ale and yule cake, the best sword dance on record from the cleverest mummers out. No doubt the elements were unpropitious; but the gentlemen appearing determined to immortalise their fame, and Mr McLeish, the photographer, having copyrighted his works, the result, embracing scenes from both plays selected, was nothing short of satisfactory at last. The excellence of Mr Marshall's pupils, and the efficiency of the Philharmonic Band, are so notorious that after saying the performance of these ladies and gentlemen, all amateurs be it remembered, was "unexceptionable," lengthened criticism is unnecessary. On Wednesday, with great judgment, but a portion of Stevens' lovely composition, "Ye spotted snakes," was given ; for however delicate the music, the glee as an accessory is too long by half. The reading was faultless ; the rich contralto of Miss Wood in the word "melody" told with delicious effect ; and as the lights were gradually dimmed, Bottom and Titania the while gracefully composed in balmy slumbers sweet at the foot of the flowery, ferny, woody scene, exquisitely painted throughout by Mr Bell (Nerissa and Puck), the whispering cadence

"So, good night, with lullaby,
Good night."

was perfectly rendered and managed ; in fact, it would have done credit to London or Paris, Dresden, Vienna, or Berlin, even Venice of former days. The musical programme was faithfully fulfilled throughout with one exception, inasmuch as at the last moment the charming duet, "I know a bank" (singularly appropriate considering the calling in life of so many of the actors), by Miss Shutt and Mr James Wilson, had to be abandoned, in consequence of the absence of the latter. The young lady, however, substituted " Bid me discourse" (Venus and Adonis) at both performances, and the audience greeted her with that rapturous applause she invariably commands. The vocalists on the occasion, led or accompanied, as the case might bo, by their accomplished master, Mr Marshall, were in reality the old church choir, and the ladies and gentlemen tendering this sweet aid were Misses Sarah and Mary Shutt, Jane Wood, Mary Simpson, Gardham, and Bennison ; Messrs Wallace, Young, Stairmand, Chapelow, Jordan, and Wetherell. The last gentleman assisted his friend at the pianoforte during the overture to " A Midsummer Night's Dream"—a piece perfectly unfitted for such an instrument in an apartment so large ; indeed, this music, so dainty for a band, fatigued the audience, and from none other than so popular a person as the performer would it have been patiently endured. The real charms of this amateur effort to commemorate the greatest poet and master of the English language unquestionably were its purely local character in the first instance, and its unlooked for perfection in the second. Everything was home-made, and everything fitted in. All the check-takers, door-keepers, and helpers generally wore of the committee or their friends, and each wore the Coventry badge. The whole entertainment resembled much more agreeable private theatricals than any public representation. Nevertheless, the order and precision observed were admirable ; and all the seats being numbered, not the smallest confusion arose. How much of our comfort depends upon attention to minor details ! Had there been any trouble about places, as there too often is—but thanks to Messrs Lee, Bailey, Potts, Heaviside, Hardy, Snaith, and the assiduous treasurer, Mr Wilkes, to whom so much is owing, Kirsop, and the Hon. Sec., there was no chance of that—it would have unsettled numbers for the whole night, and spoilt all their enjoyment. Nay, had the scene shifting been clumsy or unpunctual, which owing to the accuracy of the ever-ready and willing George Wilson, it was not, blunder after blunder would have marred the nicety of stage effect. The utmost attention was paid to subordinate parts. Nerissa, the Duke's secretary, and Salanio, in the little allotted to them, materially assisted the unity of the trial scene ; Flute, the bellows-mender, and Starveling, a tailor, looked their parts admirably ; and Mr W. Hodgson, when in piteous tones he said, " Nay, faith, let me not play a woman ; I have a beard coming !" stroking his downy chin, excited roars of laughter, so true is it—

"One touch of nature makes the whole world kin."

Other towns may have had grander pronunciations, no doubt ; but none can have been a more unalloyed success than our own. So well were all the scenes put upon the boards that on each rising of the dropscene an animated finished composition was presented, in which no artist, no critic, could detect the slightest lack of harmony in grouping or in tone. Even the chairman, Mr Elgee, who on every stage of life has a pleasant word and heartiness for all around him, in conducting the songstress of the evening towards and from the footlights, was quite a picture. If the first essay of the dramatic committee had done no more than achieve a wonderful and momentary intellectual success, the town owes thanks; but it has also created a wholesome and an agreeable impression among all classes, instructing and amusing them, while laying the foundation for future study of Shakspeare, than whom none ever so well understood the secret springs in the recesses of the human heart—he who can so deeply interest us with "The Merchant of Venice," as divert us with "A Midsummer Night's Dream," and send all home singing merrily—

> "Then heigh ho! the holly!
> The holly!
> This life is most jolly,
> Most jolly."

The result of this Tercentenary is private "Shakspeare reading clubs," and regularly organised "Amateur Dramatic Clubs," all over in England, including even Darlington, than all which nothing can have a better tendency. An admirable code of rules has been arranged for our club, the officers for which are:—
President—Fra. Mewburn, Jun. *Dramatic Manager*—J. Kendall. *Treasurer*—E. P. Elgee. *Honorary Secretary*—W. Bell. *Committee*—C. Brady, G. B. Carter, M. Frier, W. A. Snaith, J. Davis, J. W. Marshall, J. Fenwick, M. Barker, T. Potts, W. Minter, G. Wilson, and W. Smith.

P. 39 ante.

On Thursday, the 7th of April, the Darlington Choral Society gave their ninth, their most ambitious by far, and certainly most successful oratorio, to a crowded and delighted audience, in the Central Hall. At Christmas, 1856, they commenced their successful career with the Messiah, and in June of the succeeding year performed Haydn's Creation. In January following the Messiah was repeated, and on the 11th of the ensuing November Judas Maccabæus was given. In January, 1860, Samson was selected; in April, 1861, Mendelssohn's St. Paul was chosen, and in the November following Judas was repeated. In March, 1863, The Creation was repeated, and then came in 1864 the greatest effort of the highest musical genius of our day, without any exception, but with many imitators, the Elijah of the composer of St. Paul. At not one single performance has there been any failure, and the astonishing success of the society is due to the untiring energy, the patience, and the tact of Mr J. W. Marshall, with whom the musical education of its amateur members, belonging to various classes in society, has not only been a gratuitous labour of love, but an essential advantage in a social point of view to the inhabitants of Darlington generally. While the kindred societies of Stockton and Auckland are practically defunct, and that of Barnardcastle, if not in a state of absolute collapse, at any rate remains in abeyance, that over which he presides exhibits a vitality and a development truly refreshing. In consequence, therefore, of these other choral societies being unable to assist, from which on previous occasions much help flowed hither, the numbers at the last performance were lessened; but whether from this circumstance, or the thorough appreciation of the work in hand, or both in combination, there is no doubt the choruses were never either so brilliantly taken up, so accurately rendered, or so exceedingly difficult. From Stockton—whence formerly came a little rush of eager friends—but one arrived, Herr Schmüke (oboe), a German gentleman, who gave his time and his talents gratuitously. From Bishop Auckland, Mr Nicholas Kilburn, whose performance on the harmonium elicited great praise, especially in his exquisite accompaniment to the air, "For the mountains shall depart," in which he supplied the oboe part with remarkable taste and execution, and Mr Nevison, an alto in the chorus, were the only additions. From Barnardcastle there was not a single representative. The band was strengthened from Leeds and Sunderland —by none so much as Mr Wilson, of the former place, whose obligato on the violoncello to the air, "It is enough, O Lord," and Mr Tate, of the latter, who, in addition to his thorough musical knowledge and mastery over four instruments, is so accomplished a linguist as to be proficient in no less than five languages ! The principals on the occasion were Miss Helena Walker (soprano), and Mr William Dawson (tenor), both from Leeds ; Miss Crossland (contralto), Huddersfield ; and Mr Ferry (basso), of Sunderland. The last gentleman undertook the character of the Prophet, and was a host in himself, for in addition to sustaining his own arduous duties with consummate taste and faultless tune, he brought as graceful accessories to the choir his two gifted daughters. Mr Dawson possesses an organ of ringing sweetness, which he has evidently cultivated with the utmost care, under, to any other man, overwhelming discouragement, and drew down almost the most rapturous applause of the evening, in which the orchestra joined heartily, and the audience positively *demanded* the repetition of the air, "Then shall the righteous shine forth as the sun." Both ladies were suffering from catarrh, but each exerted herself admirably, and with a will deserving special notice.

I once heard Mendelssohn improvise on "The harmonious blacksmith"—fine tribute from such a man—and his oratorio of Elijah is so descriptive and dramatic a score—possessing such rhythm throughout, so much unity combined with simplicity in some parts, and the most wonderful, flashing, terrible genius in others—that it may be compared with any effort of other men, and banish comparison. Mr Ferry as the Prophet commenced with a recitative, "As God the Lord of Israel liveth"—which was immediately followed by an overture, eccentric and brilliant as to composition and situation. He tells the people, "There shall not be dew, nor rain these three years"—the overture wondrously describes the horrors of the drought—and the thirsty multitude then in chorus cry, "Help, Lord, wilt thou quite destroy us?" In their first line was the only uncertainty or flinching they showed during the evening. Confidence, however, was soon restored, and in the next, "The harvest now is over, the summer days are gone," there was nothing to be desired. "The people" then bewail that "The deeps afford no water, the rivers are exhausted; the suckling's tongue now cleaveth for thirst to his mouth ; the infant children ask for bread, and there is no one breaketh it to feed them," in a recitative chorus, one of the most so of the many original and striking beauties of the composition, which was rendered superbly. It is followed by a duett and chorus of "The People"—" Lord, bow thine ear to our prayer," plaintive to a degree. Then Obadiah (Mr Dawson) the servant of Elijah, appears on the stage, giving a recitative " Ye people rend your hearts," and the air, " If with all your hearts ye truly seek me." Here his clear silvery notes came out to perfection, and the chorus of "The People," in desperation, " Yet doth the Lord see it not ; He mocketh at us," formed one of those wonderful contrasts over which the composer had so astonishing a command. " An angel" (Miss Crossland), then warns the Prophet, " Elijah, get thee hence, Elijah !" to depart, and with a double quartett "For He shall give his angels charge over thee," the most intense interest was excited, and remained unflagging till the close of the performance. It was sustained by the four principals, assisted by Miss Ferry, and Miss Sarah Shutt, a very promising pupil of Mr Marshall, Mr John Burgin, and Mr James Wilson, than whom, with his brother, there are few steadier supporters of the society ; it produced a profound sensation, and would like many other parts have been encored, no doubt, but for the rapid flow of the composition, in which there appears no hesitation or hitch whatever. The angel (Crossland) again, " Now Cherith's brook is dried up," urges Elijah to "depart and get to Zarephath, where the Lord hath commanded a widow there to sustain him until He sendeth rain upon the earth." The widow (Miss Walker), in a recitative, " What have I to do with thee, O man of God," laments the sickness of her son, for whom she "goes mourning all the day long, and weeps at night," fears the prophet may do her harm, and slay him ; but Elijah says, "Give me thy son," and prays to the Lord to " restore the spirit of the child." The widow exclaims, " The Lord hath heard thy prayer, the soul of my son reviveth, and by this I know that thou art a man of God ;" a dialogue as dramatic as music can be ensues, and it was rendered with an ability surprising everyone. After the fine passage winding up with the chorus, " Blessed are the men who fear him," Elijah determines, " As God the Lord of Sabaoth liveth," to show himself to Ahab the King, and then he " Will send rain again upon the earth." Ahab (Mr Dawson) jeers the man of God—" Art thou Elijah ?" and " the people" unite " Thou art Elijah, thou be that troubleth Israel !" in tones the most insulting, when the Prophet magnificently declaims, " I never troubled Israel's peace ; it is thou, Ahab, and all thy father's house ;" and the chorus follows suite. Between Elijah and " the priests of Baal"—" Baal, we cry to thee"—a tremendous scene results, in which solo and chorus received, as well they deserved, immense applause. In that chorus of the Priests, " Baal hear and answer !" occurs that pause of two bars so much admired, and nothing could well be more telling than the way in which it was observed. In a beautiful recitative and air, " Draw near, all ye people ; come to me !" the Prophet implores the mercy of God on the children of Israel ; and he is supported by a quartett of angels, "Cast thy

K

burthen upon the Lord ; he shall sustain thee." In this the
four principals combined, and in the chorus of the people,
"The fire descends from Heaven," their rage turns upon the
priests, and another of those graphic contrasts occurs, render-
ing the composition so spirited and sublime. In the following
air, " Is not His word like a fire ?" Mr Ferry began a bar too
soon, but was instantly recovered by the conductor's unerring
baton, and sang the remainder of the piece to perfection, reaching with ease and vigour F natural, the same note as tenors
generally take, thus showing the extent of his register. Fine
as the voice undoubtedly is, and consummate as his execution,
it struck me that in this particular and remarkable air it lacked
the massiveness and power so requisite for its interpretation.
Obadiah and Elijah, the priests, being slain, in recitatives, "Oh,
man of God" and " O Lord, thou hast overthrown thine enemies ;" and the people, in the graceful chorus, "Open the
Heavens," then implore God to send rain, while Elijah, " Go
up now child," tells a youth (Miss Shutt) to "look toward the
sea." A dialogue follows, in which the brilliant voice of this
young lady was almost electrifying. At length she exclaims,
"Behold, a little cloud ariseth, and the rain descends." Thus
the first part closes with a chorus, "Thanks be to God: He
laveth the thirsty land," of the most wonderful descriptive and
inventive power imaginable, while exemplifying to the utmost
the care bestowed in practice. With a punctuality he always
observes, at the end of the "ten minutes" Mr Marshall was at
his post, and Miss Walker sang with exquisite expression the
air "Hear ye Israel," and the recitative, "Thus saith the
Lord." reaching A natural with equal ease and precision. A
fine chorus, " Be not afraid," as fine as anything in the book,
followed ; but, although there were two cornets in the band,
they were tame, if not actually mute, when they should
especially have come out in force. Elijah declaims, "The
Lord hath exalted thee from among the people," and tells
Ahab his wickedness, when Jezebel (Miss Crossland) reproaches
him, and the chorus agree with her. The altercation is carried
on until Elijah becomes wearied of the stiff-necked and
perverse people and their detestable queen, and in the air,
"It is enough, O Lord," desires to die. In this air Mr Ferry
surpassed himself: and the violoncello obligato accompaniment
of Mr Wilson, of Leeds, was a performance of which dear old
Lindley might have been proud. Here begins, and from this
point to the recitative chorus, "Go, return upon thy way," is
comprised, if it be possible to make a distinction of gems in the
Elijah, its finest proportion. The trio of angels (the Misses
Walker, Crossland, and Shutt), "Lift thine eyes" was thrilling,
and gained a rapturous encore ; followed by the loveliest
chorus of them all, "He, watching over Israel, slumbers not,
nor sleeps," and its execution scarcely could be exceeded. In
Elijah's next part, " O Lord, I have laboured in vain," the
trombones, like one instrument, so true was the time, came in
magnificently, as indeed they did at the close of the first part,
" Unto thee will I cry." Miss Crossland, having at this period
of the evening recovered from her hoarseness, gave the angel's
air, " O rest in the Lord," with extreme taste, her fine contralto
voice suiting the music admirably, while the flute obligato of

Mr Wetherell, a punctual amateur student in the local choir, was exceedingly fine, and gave high promise for the future of this young gentleman's career. Mr Ferry was applauded in Elijah's air, "For the mountains shall depart;" richly he deserved the compliment, and with great ability, as has been previously observed, Mr Kilburn accompanied him. When Mendelssohn first listened to this part of his composition on a full band, he wept. It precedes the mighty and dramatic chorus, "Then did Elijah, the Prophet, break forth like a fire," which concludes "Elijah went in a fiery chariot by a whirlwind to heaven," and that beautiful air, "Then shall the righteous shine forth as the sun," in which Mr Dawson took his audience by storm and gained an encore. A quartett by the principals, "O come every one that thirsteth, O come to the waters, O come unto Him;" followed amidst unsuppressed admiration, and the grand oratorio concluded with a final chorus, "And then, then shall your light break forth as the light of the morning," of jubilant and ecstatic praise and thanksgiving, like that at the close of the former part, reminding one of St. Paul, and finishing with an elaborate fugue. It is difficult to curtail any account of such a performance as this was ; for any town, even for the West Riding, it would have been a credit. The numbers engaged in the orchestra were only ninety, including the four principals, and comprising twelve tenor, seventeen treble, eighteen bass, and ten alto voices ; four first violins, including Mr Iles, a gifted youth from Leeds, and Messrs Temple and Ellis, local members, who have afforded the greatest assistance in getting up the chorus ; four second violins, two violas, three violoncellos, three contrabasses, two flutes, one oboe, two bassoons, two cornets, three trombones, harmonium, and kettledrums presided over by a remarkably clever lad from Halifax. To Messrs Sang the secretary, Harris the treasurer, and Wallace the librarian, the utmost thanks are due for their enthusiasm and attention to the interests of the society, who, with their able instructor and conductor, Mr Marshall, were heartily congratulated on their accomplished success, all of us hoping at the same time that they may never experience less deserved applause than their last achievement elicited. The number of members on the books now is 70 ; in 1861 it was 90, and the continued absence from the society of several talented amateurs in the town, one of whom particularly might take rank amongst professional violinists, is to be regretted. The audience filled every part of the Hall, and comprised among others the Rev. Dr. and Mrs Edleston, Gainford ; the Rev. E. and Mrs Cheese, Houghton ; Dr. Mackie, Mrs Coleman, Mrs Smithson, and Mrs Calverley Bewicke, Heighington; the Misses Dodgson and Mr Dodgson, Croft Rectory ; Miss Dodgson, Cockerton Hall, and her pupils; Mrs Raine, Snow Hall ; the Misses Fell, Gainford ; Mrs and Miss Scurfield, Hurworth ; Mr and Mrs Waldy, the Rev. W. H. G. and Mrs Stephens, the Rev. J. G., Mrs, and Miss Pearson ; the Rev. M. and Mrs Miller and the Revs. — Bentley and J. T. Taylor ; Dr. Clarkson, Dr. Haslewood, Mr H. K. Spark and party ; Mr and Mrs J. P. Pritchett, the Messrs and Miss Macnay and Miss Cook, Mr E. and the Misses Kipling, Mr and Mrs W. Thompson and party ; Mrs and

Miss Heslop, the Messrs and Misses Dinsdale, Mr and Mrs J. H. Bowman, Mr George Bowes and party ; Mrs Brewster, Miss Bamber and her pupils ; Mr and Mrs J. R. Fothergill, Dr. Cook, Mr and Mrs J. Marley, Mrs Marshall, Misses Booth and Misses Kilburn, Bishop Auckland ; and Messrs Moorsom, S. Russell, Bryson, C.E., T. Clayhills, Speciall, Clark, Brady, Fra. Mewburn, jun., &c., &c.

P. 40 Ante.

This entertainment was given to Mr William Hanson, on quitting the service of the Messrs Pease for that of Mr Samuelson, over whose furnaces at Newport he has now the complete management—in fact, he will be his employer's *alter ego* there, instead of the subordinate he was here. All his friends and acquaintances, if of the latter he had any who were not the former, sincerely regret his absence from the social circle, for few, very few are so great in the esteem of others as himself ; but when it is remembered he is now in a position where his exceptional talents and his willing labours will be thoroughly appreciated and handsomely requited by a gentleman in every sense of the word, there is nothing but satisfaction in a change so materially to his own advantage in all respects. His late official chief, Mr J. R. Brockon, presided, and another fellowmate, Mr C. R. Fry, occupied the vice-chair with equal ability. The evening was a very pleasant one till near its close, when the landlord sent in a *posse* of waiters to clear the decks, while the guests remained. Yorick's brother-in-law, never more gay and debonair than on that occasion, ordered them out, and hence the conception of the following prospectus, which in its extravagance is no burlesque upon those of other bubble companies of the present day :—

THE DARLINGTON HOTEL COMPANY (LIMITED).

CAPITAL, £5,000,000 STERLING, *with power to increase to* £10,000,000.

This company is formed to supply a want long felt and generally expressed, of a really superior and well-conducted hotel in the important and rapidly rising town of Darlington.

Four sites offer themselves :—one, the present King's Head, with the whole of the north side of Priestgate down to the Skerne ; another, the Sun Inn, with the D.D. Bank and Prospect Place to Bondgate, on the one hand, and as much of Northgate as may be required on the other. The third site is " Kitching's Corner," with six, eight, or ten houses right and left, as may be agreed upon ; and the fourth from the Waterloo Hotel to the Bullwynd, Houndgate, and Petty's garden inclusive, utilizing or razing the Central Hall if necessary.

That any of these properties can be obtained on reasonable terms there cannot be the slightest doubt, and it is only for the company to decide which of the four they will select.

Thus securing all the advantages that position can command ; then calling to its aid all that architecture in designing and erecting an imposing and classic front—all that liberal outlay and good taste can combine of comfort and elegance in interior decoration and arrangement—the company will be able to open to the public an establishment more than rivalling all that northern England can produce.

Nor will bricks and mortar, wood and stone, size and decoration of rooms, alone receive attention ; the staff—from manager to boots, from cook to scullery-maid—will be the object of most watchful care.

The landlord of a good hotel—the temporary home of gentlemen, men of education and of fortune—should be, as far as possible, a gentleman, too. In vain do you erect a palace, if within you are to find manners the reverse of courteous. Our manager must have the *Entree* at St. James's, and our "Boots" shall be highly polished.

THE INNER MAN.

The cuisine will be, of course, a carefully-studied feature In England, too many people know a dinner only by name—they devour food, but the reality of a good dinner is a thing unknown to them. Hence, alas! 900 of the 1,000 ills that flesh is heir to. From among the directors will be formed a committee of taste, to whom cookery has been the study of a life—men who wisely live to eat, and do not foolishly eat to live, and who will make of the Darlington Hotel more than a Greenwich "Trafalgar," a Richmond "Star and Garter," or a Saltburn "Zetland Hotel."

LUXURY.

To raise cookery to a science, and to make of eating and drinking a fine art, will not be the boundary of the company's ambition; taste will emphatically reign supreme throughout all their arrangements. Wandering through the rooms provided by the Darlington Hotel Company (limited), or reposing on its luxurious couches and divans—the eye resting on statue and statuette, on paintings, both modern and ancient, on inlaid floors and gilded cornices— the guest shall fancy himself in a gallery of art, and not merely in an inn.

ACCOMMODATION FOR THE INFERIOR CLASSES.

To secure as much profit as circumstances will admit, and at the same time to allow all classes to share in the advantage offered by the new hotel, second and third class accommodation will be provided. But this will be underground, or carefully separated from the rest of the premises by stone walls and fire brick, so that no offence may be given to the people of quality, for whom the hotel is principally provided.

VIRTUE.

The hotel will be conducted on high moral principles. No late revels will be tolerated. At a certain hour the waiters will be ordered to remove bottles, glasses, dessert, or whatever may remain on the festive board. Smoking will be relegated to a remote part of the building, and swearing will be an extra, that is to say, profane language will subject the offender to a fine. The billiard room will be conducted on principles which even a Scotchman may approve.

PHYSIC.

The Valetudinarian will be invited to seek health within the walls of the Darlington Hotel. The medicinal waters of Croft and Middleton will be brought to the premises in pipes, thus the guests may have the benefits of Spa waters and Spa baths without quitting their bedrooms. Nor will the German ocean be forgotten, as an early tank or water butt train will be provided from Redcar to bring to the hotel sea water for baths hot and cold, and fish of every imaginable variety.

WINES AND LIQUORS.

Good eating demands good drinking, and the Darlington Hotel Company (Limited) is determined to set its face against the mere "Vinter's brewings," misnamed wine, and to supply a genuine article, the real fermented juice of the grape from the days of Noah, acknowledged to be a health, strength, and joy-giving tipple. To accomplish this object, agents will be appointed in all the celebrated districts of France, the Rhine, Spain and Portugal, Hungary, &c., to make such bids as must secure the best vintages of all sorts. Thus will the wants of the highest and wealthiest class of guests be provided for; but going lower down in the social scale, and looking to the smaller means of a style of "genteel hindigence," South African sherries, and the Chancellor's shilling Tariff clarets will find a corner on the wine lists. Even the Permissive Bill man shall not be sent empty away—a damp quarter near the eaves shall be provided, in which like the "Ancient Mariner" he will find "Water, water, everywhere," "And not a drop o' drink," unless it be Whitwell and Co.'s "Quinine Champagne," for wedding breakfasts and occasions of solemn feast.

PROFITS.

A late landlord of the house, soon to cease to be the leading hotel in Darlington, was heard to say at a public dinner—"Gentlemen, I consider myself the most prosperous man in the place." This change from early position was entirely due to innkeeping. If, with such limited means of pleasing the public and securing custom, such profits could be secured, and such a position taken in a town where *some* business men have certainly made *some* profits, what may not reasonably be expected with such appliances and means as ours? 75 per cent for the first year, with no expenditure carried to capital, but everything beyond the building of the house taken to revenue, 75 per cent. is a small and reasonable figure. But on this head we need not dilate, as nearly all the shares are already taken up, and what remain will be allotted only as especial favours, and to persons likely to become good customers.

Provisional Office. —The Cattle Market, Darlington,
August, 1864.

P. 45 Ante.

In many parts of the South of England the drought has produced a disastrous dearth ; in Somersetshire and Cornwall cattle have long been fed on hay ; in the Isle of Wight water is sold at high prices for very small quantities – cattle are being driven miles for water, or it is brought great distances to them. Even here, in South Durham, where we don't suffer so much, the Tees is so low that there is no flow over the Dinsdale fish lock. Mr E. J. Lowe, writing from Highfield-house Observatory, (Aug 10), says the drought has been severely felt there, many shrubs and herbaceous plants having died. The hay crop was gathered with scarcely a drop of rain, the quantity deficient, and at the present moment the corn harvest is general. The following is the rainfall for 1864 :—

	Amount, inches.			Amount, inches.
January	0 74	May	..	1·29
February	1·50	June	..	1·26
March..	2·56	July	..	0·52
April	2·08			
		Total	.. ..	9·95

In May, June, and July, the deficiency has amounted to four inches. Up to July 31, 124 days were without rain.

In Sussex the rainfall for the last eight years in the three months of each year, corresponding with those of this drought up to July, is :—

Year.	May.	June.	July.	Total.
1857 ..	.. 1·57	.... 1·95	.... 1·10	.... 4·62
1858 ..	.. 1·77	.... 0·17	.... 3·16	.... 5·04
1859 ..	.. 1·13	.... 1·52	.... 1·11	.... 3·76
1860 ..	.. 3·65	.... 4·73	.... 3·50	.... 11·03
1861 ..	.. 1·93	.... 3·53	.... 2·65	.... 8·11
1862 ..	.. 3·53	.... 2·37	.... 1·95	.... 7·75
1863 ..	.. 2·39	.... 4·11	.... 0·60	.... 7·17
1864 ..	.. 1·21	.... 1·19	.... 0·55	.... 3·65

It will be seen, therefore, that this year we have had less rain than in the dry season of 1859. July of 1863 was nearly as dry as this, but the ground was better prepared, having over four inches in June. At Diss, in Norfolk (August 12th), when we had a very close day following a hot night, the *mini-*

mum temperature in the morning was 32·5 deg. At 5 a m. the
ground was covered with white frost, and ice the thickness of
common window-glass was found on shallow troughs. That
day week the greatest heat in the shade was 88·5 deg. Thus
we have a range of 56 deg. in little over a week's time.

After all, I find the crops will reach the average. In Scotland
the turnips are excellent, and the harvest as forward as, if not
more so than, in the best parts of the North of England, and
nothing can exceed the loveliness of the weather we are enjoying in Argyleshire and the Hebrides. The following table is
interesting : —

RAINFALL IN THE BRITISH ISLES.

Stations.	February to July inclusive.		June and July.		July, 1864.
	1863.	1864.	1863.	1864.	
	Inches.	Inches.	Inches.	Inches.	Inchs.
Camden-town, London	9·21	8·12	5·78	2·29	·61
Selborne ..	9·93	10·18	5·03	1·49	·36
Banbury ..	8·25	10·53	5·16	2·33	·88
Wisbeach	6·92	8·25	3 76	1·67	·55
Calne	9·88	8·72	5·11	2·34	·67
Goodamoor, Plymouth	20·82	13·85	8·34	4·42	1·63
Taunton ..	9·67	9·13	4·50	1·87	·70
Orleton, Tenbury	9·57	11·90	5·52	4·50	2·64
Wigston, Leicester	7·63	9·40	4·33	1·66	·30
West Retford ..	6·02	11·88	4·13	2·75	1·01
Manchester	11·11	15·45	6·26	4·64	1·70
North Shields ..	8·86	13·04	4·85	2·77	·85
Seathwaite, Cumberland	60·63	49·01	13·83	19·19	7·57
Haverfordwest ..	12·57	12·19	5·01	5 61	2·90
Dumfries..	14·47	10·84	4·77	4·55	1·55
Oban	26·93	23·65	5·25	8·65	3·05
Danston, Perthshire ..	15·65	20·47	3·65	7·69	3·85
Aberdeen	9·12	13·54	3·10	3·75	2·26
Culloden, Inverness ..	9·21	11·56	2·25	3·57	1·90
Portree, Isle of Skye ..	47·54	36·45	8·02	12·08	4·66
Sandwick, Orkney	13 81	13·11	2·30	3·53	1·63
Cork	11·64	11·83	5·37	2·76	·70
Killaloe, Clare ..	16·73	12 82	4·04	5·03	1·64
Portarlington	15·46	13·05	5·35	2·01	·79
Monkstown, Dublin ..	7·59	9·33	3·14	2·01	·68
Galway ..	24·52	23·78	5·59	8·42	3·01
Waringstown, Down ..	8·80	11·26	2 88	3·79	1·15
Leckpatrick, Strabane	15·09	17·21	6·39	6·05	2·56

RAILWAY STATISTICS.

The vast importance of the railway system cannot be exaggerated. The struggles during its gestation, owing to the
prejudice of ignorance, or the strength of opposing interests,
are now matters of curious history. The original Stockton
and Darlington line, 25 miles in length, was opened September
27th, 1825. In first estimating the revenue passengers were
not taken into consideration at all—what the old one-horse
coach conveyed being an inconsiderable item. The original
calculation was :—

165,488 tons of coal	..........£11,904	19	0
2,000 ,, lime	....	104 13	0
Merchandise..................	4,000	0	0

£16,000 12 0

Yet, for the year ending June 30th, 1827, the gross income stood :—

Coals	£14,455	5	2
Lime	1,026	16	10
Merchandise	1,240	4	1
Passengers	563	14	0
Sundries	1,018	3	6
	£18,304	4	4

So much for the shrewdness and justification of the speculation ; but comparing that period with the present, knowing the amazing results of the development of that system, the Parliamentary paper issued on the 4th of August, is of prodigious interest. It states :—During the year 1863 there were in England and Wales 12 passengers killed and 371 injured from causes beyond their own control ; and 13 killed and 1 injured from their own misconduct or want of caution. There were 7 servants of companies or contractors killed, and 29 injured from causes beyond their own control ; 66 killed, and 12 injured from their own misconduct. Five were killed at level crossings ; 25 trespassers were killed, and 4 injured. There were one person killed, and 2 injured from miscellaneous causes. In Scotland the figures were—passengers killed from causes beyond their own control, 2 ; injured, 11 ; from their own misconduct, killed, 6 ; servants killed from causes beyond their own control, 4 ; injured, 12 ; from their own misconduct, killed, 11 ; injured, 2 ; killed at level crossings, 1 ; injured, 1 ; trespassers killed, 8 ; injured, 1 ; miscellaneous, injured, 1. Ireland —Passengers killed from causes beyond their own control, 0 ; injured, 18 ; killed from their own misconduct, 2 ; servants injured from causes beyond their own control, 3 ; killed from their own misconduct, 10 ; killed at level crossings, 3 ; trespassers killed, 7 ; injured, 2 ; miscellaneous, killed, 1. The number of miles open in England and Wales, on the 31st of December last, was double, 5,876 ; single, 2,692—total, 8,568. The number of passengers, exclusive of season-ticket holders, was—first-class, 21,992,216 ; second, 51,794,959 ; third, 99,818,310 ; total, 173,605,485. The season-ticket holders were 42,991. The number of passenger trains was 2,396,334, which ran 50,515,081 miles ; goods trains, 1,415,524, which ran 46,909,098 ; total, 3,811,878 trains, which ran 97,424,179 miles. The receipts from first-class passengers were £2,868,221 (a slight diminution) ; second, £3,773,684 ; third £3,048,774 ; season tickets, £287,956 ; total, £10,878,635. Receipts for excess of luggage, horses, dogs, &c., £992,570 ; mails, £391,211. Total from passenger traffic, £12,262,416 ; live stock, £465,154 ; minerals, £4,504,434 ; general merchandise, £8,980,818. Total goods traffic, £13,950,406 ; total receipts for traffic, £26,212,822. The total receipts in Scotland were £3,424,921 ; and in Ireland, £1,518,654. The proportion of expenditure to receipts last year was 48 per cent., the proportion in 1862 having been 49. The total amount of capital paid up on the 31st of December was £404,215,525 ; and the net receipts were £16,048,931, which would yield an average return of something less than 4 per cent.

Robertson and Calvert, Printers, Saddler Street, Durham.